WHO AM I REALLY?

By Damon L. Davis

PROLOGUE

THE ADOPTION of a child is a very complicated process to fully comprehend; unless you've lived through one, you probably don't fully understand. The adoption process is said to be a triad of participants: birth parents, adoptees, and adopted parents. But I believe adoption is a combination of far more. Every person, adoptee or otherwise, is molded by their immediate and extended family, their broader community and its belief systems, and myriad other factors too numerous to name. On my podcast, *Who Am I Really?* (www.WhoAmIReallypodcast.com), I've spoken to dozens of adoptees about their experiences in adoption and their attempts to reunite with their biological family members.

On the show I've learned there are countless complicating factors in every person's life and adoption as a life's journey takes on many forms. My podcast guests talk about the ways their adoptive parents tried to make sure they felt comfortable with their adoption. Some parents buy books on the subject to read with their children, explaining that they are loved and attempting to make them feel special for being chosen for adoption. Often, adopted children do feel comforted that they were special enough to be chosen, but sometimes they wonder why they weren't special enough to be kept and raised by their own parents.

Guests have shared stories of transracial adoptions, in which parents of one race adopt a child from another race. I've heard tales of people adopted into certain global cultures or religions who feel very little connection to that upbringing, always sensing that they were someone else deep inside. Others feel a different kind of disconnect from their adoptive family, like being an artistic, free-spirited, creative person in a family of rule-following straight arrows. Some people have said they felt extroverted in an introverted family, or they just saw the world differently than their adoptive parents and siblings. Sometimes the differences are physical, like skin tone or height and weight. But one of the worst scenarios for other adoptees is having unsupportive, even abusive adoptive parents who overtly or intentionally reminded the adoptee that they were the biological child of someone else.

Searching for our relatives is an adventure unto itself. I've heard amazing tales of people's searches for their first family back in pre-internet days. Those stories are amazing to me, as adoptees recount the true detective work they had to do. They share tales of numerous appeals to the court system to release their documents, diligent, even desperate, searches through library archives for clues, or tracking down phone numbers for people they hope are the family members they're seeking.

Today, technology allows a new generation of adoptees to connect more quickly and locate clues more easily than ever before. Reunion registries allow people to broadcast their search to anyone who will listen online; vast networks of "Search Angels" are volunteering to aid a person's investigation, because they know how important it is for some adoptees to reconnect with family members. Social networks like Facebook make it easy to search for people yourself on lunch breaks and after hours, allowing adoptees to peek into the personality—or even see a photo—of someone they have a connection to. Even more incredibly, the proliferation of commercialized DNA testing companies, like AncestryDNA and 23andMe, are giving adoptees scientific proof of their biological connection to distant relatives—or directly to their birth parents.

Finally, the reunion itself can be a harrowing experience. Some people are welcomed by one or both birth parents who've remembered that person's life ever since their child was sent off into the world. Others are summarily rejected by parents who feel that they dealt with that chapter of their life years ago and are appalled—even offended—that the adoptee would step forward and reopen that chapter; they've moved on. Still others embark on the journey to find their birth parents only to learn that they're deceased. Some adoptees have a strong feeling their parent is already gone, even before they learn the facts; others learn their parent passed away very recently, making the pain at the end of their search more acute, because they just barely missed meeting their loved one. Of course, sometimes there are new sibling relationships to navigate as well. Some adoptees learn their biological parents stayed together after their adoption, and they have full-blood siblings. Sometimes, a person has half siblings, some of whom are eager to meet them, and others who want nothing to do with them.

There are components of the adoption journey that I haven't even touched on here. Social workers, foster families, biological relatives and other influencers are huge parts of the adoption constellation. Of course, every birth parent also has their own full story to tell about why and how an adoption plan was made for their child.

Furthermore, adoptees also have to navigate the feelings of their adopted parents about their desire to search, making sure they know they're not being replaced, the search is purely a quest for answers.

That nagging curiosity is often the catalyst for an adoptee's search for their first family. If you're not adopted, try to imagine for yourself that you've been told you're directly related to other parents and siblings whom you don't know. It's almost inevitable that you would develop a curiosity about who those people could be. We're curious about birth parents' personalities and physical traits, and which pieces of ourselves we inherited from them. Adoptees are hungry for information about their medical history and the mysteries contained within. For any person battling a hereditary chronic illness, or caring for a loved one who is, you understand the dire importance of having as much information as possible, like family health history.

Who Am I Really?

I've shared these scenarios to introduce the adoption experience, at the highest level, and to help anyone who is not directly impacted by adoption to empathize with adoptees. I've lived two of the three sides of the triad. I'm an adoptee and an adoptive parent, so I know the triumphs and struggles of adoption all too well. I hope, that after learning my story, adoptees will feel inspiration for the possibilities of their own reunions, even in the face of adversity.

Reading my journey, I want adoptive parents to understand some of the love, gratitude, and consideration an adoptee might have for them as their parents. I hope they will appreciate hearing the inner thoughts an adoptee might have when considering reunion with birth parents. My hope is that birth parents will also understand some of the thoughts and emotions that an adoptee contemplates and experiences when we consider reunion with you, and what we feel in the aftermath of learning facts about our adoption or our natural family tree.

I've been so lucky to research the lives of my biological parents and adopted parents during the years before my adoption. It put the path of my life, culminating in our reunions, into perspective. I want to thank: Veronica's sister Bonnie Akins; Willie's lifelong friend Waymon Guinn; my biological cousins Mary Ann Dussent and Marla Owens; Ann's lifelong friend Schelley Kiah; Ann's graduate school friend Sharon Holley; and Christine Owens Boone for their recollections of the past. I also want to thank my family and friends for supporting me throughout my journey to this point in my life. I love you all, more than you know.

As I write this "Who Am I Really?' is approaching 100 adoptees who will have shared their journeys on the show. I've been humbled by the trust others have placed in me to help share their personal stories. Now it's my turn.

This is for Seth, and everyone who follows him…

CONTENTS

CHAPTER 1 Michael 9

CHAPTER 2 Ann 15

CHAPTER 3 Bill 27

CHAPTER 4 Veronica 33

CHAPTER 5 Willie 47

CHAPTER 6 Damon—Columbia, MD 53

   I Knew My In-Laws Before I Met My Wife 64

   The Adoptee Adopts 69

CHAPTER 7 Seth 75

CHAPTER 8 Happy to Be at Home 83

CHAPTER 9 The Search 87

CHAPTER 10 "36 Years…" 105

   The Birthday Surprise 115

CHAPTER 11 The End of Five Incredible Years in Reunion 131

CHAPTER 12 Suddenly Willie Davis Was Gone 147

CHAPTER 13 The Mistaken Identification of Mr. H 161

CHAPTER 14 "Many a mile has been traversed and there are miles to go." 173

CHAPTER 15 END 201

CHAPTER 1

MICHAEL

WITHIN SECONDS of my first breath on October 14, 1972, the birthing staff at Baltimore's Union Memorial Hospital whisked me away from my mother. Under normal circumstances, a newborn infant is placed on his mother's bare chest to begin the intimate skin-on-skin bonding that unites a mother with her child outside of her womb. There would be no bonding between me and my mother that day. I was extracted from her body through a vertical Cesarean section (C-section) incision on her lower abdomen. We were separated immediately, following the staff's execution plan for infants entering adoption. For the rest of her life, the young mother would bear the physical and mental scars from the birth of a child she had carried for nine months, never met, and might never see again. I had no voice in the adoption planning, no choice in the matter. Even if I wanted to stay with her, I couldn't say so.

Ann Sullivan left the hospital to recover from her C-section surgery. I stayed in the facility for a few days before transitioning to a foster home for several months, and then to my adopted family. The plans for my life and my birth mother's life, respectively, were unknown. The only certainty was that we would not go forth together.

Who Am I Really?

A few months prior to my birth, in June of 1972, a young newlywed couple from the Midwest—Willie and Veronica Davis—had just moved to Maryland, and they were ready to start a family. Struggling with infertility, they decided to adopt a baby. The adoption referral service they called in Baltimore, Maryland ultimately connected them to Baltimore City Social Services. Their caseworker, Carolyn, scheduled an appointment for the couple to meet her at her office in the city for their first interview. In the meeting, she asked them background questions about why they wanted to adopt. She described the adoption process in Maryland and gave them personal questionnaires to be completed at home and returned to her later. The preliminary paperwork included budget forms—and medical forms, which their respective physicians had to complete.

In September 1972, Carolyn met with the young couple again. This time, she went to see them at their small apartment in Columbia, Maryland. She asked more questions about their feelings for one another, their respective families, and of course, how they felt about adopting a child. They must have given satisfactory answers showing they were worthy of parenthood, because the couple was approved for adoption in November.

In early January 1973, Carolyn called Veronica at work with the good news; she and her husband had been matched with an infant. The baby boy they'd wished they could have together had been delivered by a young mother in Baltimore, back in October. She had made an adoption plan, and Willie and Veronica were given the chance to have a son. In the days after the call, the couple drove to the adoption agency to hear pieces of my history and see a photograph of me. They knew immediately from the photo that they wanted to make a family with me. On February 26, 1973, the couple returned to the adoption agency to meet me for the first time. We spent about one hour together that day. The very next day, February 27, Willie and Veronica—Mom and Dad—

took me home to our apartment at 5470 Harper's Farm Road, Columbia, MD. They became my loving parents.

It's common in infant adoptions for the adoptive parents to change the birth name their son or daughter was given to a new name. That practice helps, for better or worse, to de-identify the child from their prior life, and attempts to bond the child to their new parents through a new identity. Some children destined for adoption are never given a birth name, so the name they grow up with as an adoptee is the only identity they've ever had. When Ann gave birth to me, and for the first five months of my life, my name was Michael. When I was adopted my parents named me Damon, and that is who I am.

I've always known I was an adoptee, from as young as I can remember. Mom and Dad were open and transparent with me about the meaning of adoption from an early age. When I was a little boy, my mother gave me a laminated piece of paper with a short story about adoption on it that comforted me about how our family was formed. It read something like this:

> *One day, an elementary school class was talking about families. The teacher asked the children about each of their families, and one child answered that they were adopted. Another child asked what* adopted *meant. The adopted child said, "It means I was born in my mother's heart, not in her belly."*

I liked that story. It was comforting for me to imagine the universal symbol of love, a heart shape, and that my parents thought of me as a child of their love. I kept that small piece of paper in my desk drawer at home for many years.

Mom also kept a baby book with a few notes about my adoption that I could read any time I liked, but I rarely felt the need to review those notes. She had already told me the story of my adoption, and I was comfortable with the little bit I knew: I was born in Baltimore; my mother was a librarian, and my father was a police officer. Those details were good enough for me for a long time. The subject of adoption rarely arose in our home. It may have been that my parents and I looked enough alike that we passed easily as a biological family. Mom is a fair-skinned African-American woman. Dad had darker skin of the same descent. My skin tone is brown, in between theirs, so in relative terms I look like I could be their biological son. To me, there were very few differences between us. My parents and I even have the same astrological sign; we're all Libras, with birthdays in the middle of October. We're *family*. They've showered me with affection and support throughout my life. I am their only child, and they are my parents.

Growing up, occasionally Mom and I would talk about my future, and she would enquire about my aspirations when I got older. She would casually insert into those chats that if I ever wanted to talk about my adoption we could. She also suggested that if I ever wanted to search for my birth mother, when I was older, she would help me. But for many years, I never wanted to search; her open support helped me feel comfortable with who I was. I think open honesty with an adoptee from the beginning is the correct path for any family to grow together.

In time, however, I received reminders that there was another family out there that I was biologically related to. In the adoption community, adoptees refer to the awakening that you're biologically related to other parents as "coming out of the fog," or facing the reality of what adoption actually means. It took me several years to launch a search for them. Before I did, I had to think deeply about what I was getting myself into, and whom my journey might affect. I had to prepare myself for every possibility, simultaneously recognizing that I could try to imagine hundreds of scenarios and still never be prepared for reality. I wrote this book to share my adoption journey as fully as possible. It's about more than my adoption and attempts at reunion. I wrote this to share the full story of myself and some of the people and places that I hold dear. I've tried to introduce you to my birth parents, my adoptive parents, my children, and a few of the friends and family who've been with me on this incredible journey. They're all integral to understanding who I am, and how I got to this point in my life.

Everyone's adoption story is very different. This is my journey.

CHAPTER 2

ANN

MY BIOLOGICAL grandfather, James Arthur Sullivan, was fortunate to attend college at all. He graduated in 1939 from Hampton Institute, with a degree in carpentry. He moved his young family from Harrodsburg, Kentucky to the eastern shore of Maryland after landing a job teaching carpentry at Maryland State College, another historically black college/university (HBCU) like his alma mater. From then on, his daughters, Adeline (Addie) and her younger sister Ann, would grow up on Maryland State's campus in the care of their mother, Cecile, a stay-at-home mother by James' request. Addie called their mother "Momma," but Ann referred to her as "Mother." "Momma could make a penny cry, and she could make a soup out of *anything*," Addie told me many years later, referring to her mother's ability to maximize the value of the few dollars the family earned. James' meager salary forced her to be resourceful, but Cecile didn't like living in the college's staff housing in the backwoods of the school's campus.

The children got used to campus life quickly. Addie and Ann spent a lot of time exploring the vast outdoors around their home. Before long, Ann befriended another young girl, Pat Kiah, whose family also lived on campus. Pat's grandfather was president of the college; he taught classes and oversaw the school's transition to what is now the University of

Maryland Eastern Shore (UMES). But those historical accolades meant nothing to the girls back then. They each had a new friend to romp around with, in a wonderland of trees to climb and land to explore. It was a safe haven for all kinds of antics. They rode bicycles on back country roads and played outside all day until the sun went down. Their group of friends on campus was small, but they had a lot of fun growing up.

Pat recalled for me that growing up on campus was a double-edged sword. One edge was the safe outdoor environment and small, close-knit group of friends. The sharper edge sliced them with jealousy from some of their friends who lived in the surrounding community. The town of Princess Anne was a working-class community of factory workers, fishermen, and farmers. Of course, the campus kids did have some good friends in the community, with whom they attended school. However, they were sometimes ostracized because of their status as children of educated, well-spoken blacks. They were considered elites, and often the children from town expressed their envy with off-color remarks at school, reminding them of their differences.

Ann was a very light-skinned African-American girl with "flaming" red hair. She was an artistic child who took ballet, tap, and modern dance. She wrote poetry in her composition books about the beauty of rain, the strength of elephants, and the joy of Christmas. A studious young lady, she graduated second in her high school class; that academic prowess, mixed with her artistic expressions, made her an attractive candidate to college admissions officers. After high school, Ann attended Hampton University, like her father before her.

The small-town girl was on her own for the first time and enjoying the college experience—too much. After one semester of excessive socializing, playing double-deck pinochle and not studying very hard, Ann failed her classes at Hampton and returned home to the scolding of her father. He told Ann that if she wanted to continue her collegiate studies, she would have to find the money and pay for school herself. So, that's exactly what she did. Ann spent the summer of 1967 working at a Kroger's grocery store in Harrodsburg, Kentucky, beginning the process of pinching her pennies and collecting her thoughts to return to college one day.

She turned 21 years old in September 1967 and felt more mature than she had on her first try with college. Ann applied to attend another HBCU, known as Kentucky State College at that time, in Frankfort, Kentucky. Embarrassed by her past mistakes and determined to get her education, Ann was much more dedicated and studious at KSC. After her first year of school, Ann stayed at KSC to attend summer school, trying to make up for lost time in her studies. Doing great, she thought she was on track to graduate in May 1970. Unbeknownst to her, she was accidentally one credit short of graduation, pushing the end of her college career to May 1971.

In August, Ann pressed on to graduate studies in library sciences at Wayne State University in Detroit. In 1971, the city was bottoming out of its former status as one of the nation's premier cities, becoming one of its most hopeless. By then, the volatile automobile industry was suffering in the decades after its factories churned out the war machines of World War II. The racial riots of the long hot summer of 1967 had left the urban metropolis scarred, and the city's murder rate was rising. The city's Caucasian population was fleeing to the suburbs. Even the famous music industry icon Motown Records had decamped for Los Angeles.

Wayne State was launching an experimental program, the Public Library Service for the Urban Disadvantaged, intended to teach students to be librarians in public libraries located in urban settings. Only twenty students were accepted into the trial program, and Ann was one of them. The small size of the program created a close community of students who took classes separate from the university's other library sciences students. Ann's friend and fellow WSU student, Sharon Holley, told me some of those students felt like guinea pigs, but they understood the needs they would fulfill when they graduated.

Who Am I Really?

Students in the program who were native to Detroit commuted from their homes in the city. The out-of-towners lived on campus in the dormitories as roommates and suite mates. Many of the African-American students coalesced into a group that attended classes together, ate lunches together, and socialized at night and on weekends. One of the male students who lived in Detroit, a little older than the rest, occasionally opened his home to the others for a relaxing getaway. He invited them over on Sundays to watch professional football on television. On January 16, 1972, the crew gathered at his house to watch the Dallas Cowboys defeat the Miami Dolphins (24-3) in Super Bowl VI, held at Tulane Stadium in New Orleans. That game still holds the distinction of being the coldest championship game ever played.

One of Ann's friends from Maryland, Ronald Waters, also lived in the Motor City and introduced her to some of his friends. After Super Bowl weekend, Ron took Ann to a singles party, where she met a Detroit police officer she really liked. They were fond of one another and in the days after the party, they dated briefly. After an incident in which he took advantage of her, Ann ended their relationship. But she didn't achieve the clean break she'd hoped for, because very soon, Ann learned she was pregnant; the cop was the father. Ann was far from home, alone, with no money, and getting pregnant was not part of her plans. When she notified the cop that she was pregnant, he said he would help her. His pledge was hollow, however, and he didn't support Ann at all. She couldn't get in touch with the man in the days after she broke the news, and she was getting desperate. She called his police precinct to plead for his support. When the precinct operator answered the phone, Ann politely asked to speak with the man. The operator agreed to try to locate him to connect the call, asking Ann, "Is this his wife calling?" Ann's heart sank when she accidentally learned the true desperation of her situation; the father of her unborn child was a married man.

Thankfully, Ann took the time to write down some of her thoughts and feelings about that time in her life. Below is a piece of her story in her own words.

> Ann:
>
> "I was a small-town girl going to graduate school in the big city when I realized that I was pregnant, about six months from the completion of my master's degree. I was far from home and family, facing a situation that I had not expected. I had received a one year, federally-funded fellowship and was six months from graduation.
>
> "After several attempts to get help from the birth father, I accepted that I was on my own. My hope was to secure a job and start working before I delivered my child, but It was 1972; single pregnant women were not what the job market was looking for. After several interviews while attending a professional convention, I knew I had to come up with another plan. I had to finish my degree, deliver my baby, and then find a job."

Back on campus, Ann did everything she could to hide her pregnancy from her friends in the library sciences program. But she was gaining weight with each passing week; as her figure expanded, her situation became more noticeable. Ann wore larger, heavier clothes than were seasonable for the summer heat of 1972. Unable to hide her plight any longer, Ann eventually confessed her pregnancy to her friend Sharon. Their graduation from the library sciences program was approaching fast, happening in August. But Ann knew that she could not return home to Maryland as an expectant mother. Addie had gotten pregnant ten years earlier, in 1962, and that news did not sit well with their father. He had sent Addie to Baltimore and told her not to call him again until she was married. If he treated Addie that way, how would he react after Ann failed out of Hampton for being irresponsible, then returned home from graduate school pregnant with no prospects for employment?

When Ann called her lifelong friend Pat to confess her dire situation, they agreed Baltimore was the best place for her to go. Pat had just moved from Pittsburgh to Baltimore a month earlier and was employed as a social worker. It was the perfect career to support her dear friend's pregnancy, granting her access to public assistance programs and resources that Ann desperately needed. When she completed her courses at Wayne State, Ann fled Detroit and never looked back. She stayed with Pat and her husband for nearly a month while they concocted the plan for Ann to secretly deliver me in Baltimore, arrange my adoption, and smooth the whole thing over unnoticed.

Sharon had offered to let Ann move into her small apartment in Buffalo, NY after graduation. Ann thanked Sharon for her generous offer, explaining she was making plans to move to Baltimore. However, since one of Ann's goals was to keep her pregnancy a secret, Sharon served as an alibi for why she wasn't returning to Princess Ann. Saying she was in Buffalo was perfect; if Ann's parents knew she was living in Baltimore, they would certainly go visit her. Ann told her parents she was in Buffalo with Sharon, looking for a job, and gave her parents Sharon's telephone number. Whenever Ann's parents called Sharon's apartment, she always had an excuse for why they couldn't speak with Ann. "She's not in right now, but I expect her back later. I'll tell her that you called," Sharon would say. She would immediately hang up and call Ann in Baltimore to relay the message, urging a prompt call home.

Ann:

"As I approached the completion of my thesis, I contacted a childhood friend, Pat (Schelley) Kiah, who was a social worker in Baltimore. I told her of my situation and asked for her assistance. Like a true friend, she assisted me in getting help through the welfare system to find a place to live, a doctor, and a hospital where my baby could be born and placed in adoption.

"At the end of the academic year I quietly slipped away from the friends I had made and boarded a plane to Baltimore. There, I was met by my friend Pat, who helped me through each step of the process leading to a modestly furnished studio apartment, food stamps, an obstetrician, and moral support.

"I had arranged a cover story with the help of my friend Sharon, who lived in Buffalo. I told my parents that I was working in Buffalo and rooming with Sharon. When they wanted to reach me, they called Sharon. I was conveniently not at home, or unavailable. Then Sharon would call me and tell me to call home. This was before caller ID, so the plan worked."

That charade went on for a while, but the facade they crafted would eventually be revealed.

Ann:

"I spent most of my time in my studio apartment. I was without transportation, and I did not know the city. There was a small neighborhood market a block away where I could buy some groceries. It was a short walk, and I would buy only what I could carry.

"I knew I needed exercise, but I did not know the neighborhood, so I chose to walk in my apartment. I placed the TV in the best available spot and slowly walked in circles, watching television until I was tired. It was the year of the Summer Olympics in Munich Germany, and the attack on the Olympic Village that resulted in the killing of members of the Israeli Olympic team. It was a frightening time to be away from friends and family, so I talked to my constant companion, my unborn child."

There was a lot on Ann's mind and plenty of time to think about everything in her tiny apartment. Foremost in her thoughts was keeping herself healthy to deliver her baby, with maintaining the secrecy of her pregnancy a close second. In Baltimore, her proximity to her home town was fraught with the peril of running into someone she knew from back home; her worst fear was about to come true.

One day, Ann was strolling along the sidewalk near her apartment when she heard her name bellowed behind her. "*Ann!*" the voice called again, this time even closer. Her fiery red 1970's afro probably stood out in a blaze of color on the city streets, and someone had definitely recognized her. She panicked, knowing she had to make a quick escape or there would be no way to hide her bulging, pregnant belly from the man boldly shouting down the street at her. The man declared, "Ann Sullivan, I know that's you!" Her pace quickened to the highest speed a pregnant lady could maintain without running. Ann reached the entrance to her building, hustled to throw the front door open, and ducked inside without ever glancing back.

Her persistent pursuer was a man from back home in Princess Anne, MD. Feeling certain about whom he had seen, the man told his mother back east about the incident, and mentioned that Ann appeared, even at a distance, to be pregnant. Naturally, the grapevine spread the information quickly, from his mother to Ann's mother Cecile. She never said a word to her daughter about the rumor she had heard, allowing Ann's secret to remain her own. However, sometime later, Cecile told her friends she thought she had a grandchild out there somewhere.

On October 14, 1972, Ann made her way to Union Memorial Hospital to give birth. She could see the bright lights of Memorial Stadium through the window as the nurses prepared her for delivery. The child Ann spoke to and prayed for was about to embark on a separate path in life, as her plan to secure a future for the child forged ahead. When her C-section procedure was over, the delivery team asked her what to name the baby boy. "Michael Anthony Sullivan" was written down for the original birth certificate, and I was taken away. Some time later, Pat went to the hospital and asked to see me, but the hospital staff wouldn't allow it. Pat escorted Ann back to her apartment to begin her recovery.

In the wake of the life-changing delivery, Ann moved out of her tiny apartment. She no longer qualified for public assistance and needed to try to move on with her life. She moved in with her sister Addie, in Baltimore, who didn't know Ann had been living in town nor that she'd been pregnant. Ann soon admitted the ordeal she had endured over the past year to her older sister. When she shared that the child she had delivered was likely in foster care as part of her adoption plan, Addie cried. She was very upset with her younger sister for keeping her pregnancy a secret, and for putting me up for adoption. She was incredulous that Ann thought it was a better plan to have the child adopted by strangers than to find a way to raise and love the child herself. At the time, Addie was married with an eight-year-old daughter, Mary Ann; they would have welcomed the addition of a boy to the family. Addie felt confident they could have navigated the tough times together. Ann's spirit sank, and her heart and mind were torn between her decision to relinquish her son and Addie's belief that together, the family could have made it all work.

Ann's mind reeled. She started rethinking things, seriously contemplating reversing her decision and finding a way to provide for herself and her son. Ann wanted me back. As the holiday season approached, her imagination ran wild with the thought of experiencing future Christmases and other milestones in our lives together. Ann hoped that the Christmas of 1973 might be our first. But her intoxication with the mirage of the future was sobered by the reality that with each passing day, the little boy she'd sent into adoption was bonding with his new family. If they were loving him the way she desperately hoped they would, taking him back would unfairly rip their family apart. Ann reconciled with the decision she had made and looked to her future. Never forgetting her son, Ann continued to fantasize about bringing Michael home for the next several years.

In 1975, Ann was employed as a library cataloger at Delaware State University. There she met Daniel Scott, a U.S. Air Force (USAF) man stationed at Dover Air Force Base. Their relationship moved at lightning speed; just one month later, in March, Dan and Ann were married. By July of 1975, the couple had moved to Zaragoza, Spain to fulfill Dan's next USAF duty assignment. In 1979, he was reassigned to Wiesbaden, Germany, where Ann would work in the base library.

Wherever they were in the world, Ann and Pat tried their best to stay in contact and visit one another. They wrote letters back and forth, sharing how things were going in their lives. After marrying Dan, Ann's letters took a turn as she expressed her laments; the life she had settled for was draining her. She felt Dan was a possessive alcoholic, which made her very unhappy with their relationship. She couldn't figure out why she was putting up with her living situation, but she felt she lacked the strength to exit the relationship and fend for herself. Ann's self-esteem was very low, she was severely overweight, and her mental state was volatile. Pat replied to Ann's missive with disbelief, agreeing that she was not living the joyous married life the two women had dreamed for themselves in their youth. From Pat's point of view, Ann's wings had been clipped.

Ann and Dan returned to the United States and drove cross-country to Beale Air Force Base in California, mutually suffering along the way in their dying marriage. By 1978, mourning the loss of her father, stressed by the rigors of her failing marriage, and feeling unfulfilled by the trajectory of her life, Ann plotted to run away from it all. Fed up and distraught, she wrote a note in her journal that she was even contemplating suicide. She had hit bottom and desperately needed to escape. In 1980, Ann and Dan separated. When they divorced in 1985, Ann moved back to Baltimore. Her sister Addie had moved to Kentucky to care for their elderly mother, but Ann's niece Mary Ann was still there, and she was happy to have Aunt Ann nearby.

In 1986, Ann was out for the night in Baltimore with one of her girlfriends and they decided to catch a movie. They bought tickets to see the motion picture everyone was talking about, *The Color Purple*. In the film, the character of Celie, portrayed by Actress Whoopie Goldberg, struggled to find her own identity in rural Georgia in the 1930's. Her abusive father had impregnated her several times and abducted their children, whom Celie never saw again. As Ann sat in the theater with her friend, she could feel Celie's pain for the loss of her children. It was all too familiar for Ann. She had no idea that the end of the movie would be too much to bear and push her over the edge.

In the final scene, Celie had aged many years. The travails of her life were finally in the past, after decades of abuse. As she descended the steps of the front porch of her home, she saw the adult figures of her long-lost children approaching in the distance. Celie's little sister, who had escaped their abusive home years before, brought Celie's other children back to Georgia to introduce each one to their mother. The powerful scene of long-lost children reuniting with their mother overtook Ann, overwhelming her with a tsunami of emotions she had buried deep within herself. She cried uncontrollably and inconsolably in the theater for so long that her friend decided it was best to leave her there until she could gather herself. Hollywood had portrayed the reunion Ann had always hoped for.

"I was living in a secret state of vicarious mourning for my own loss—my son placed in adoption."

—Ann Sullivan

While Ann waited patiently year in and year out for a reunion similar to the one she'd witnessed on the big screen, another reunion she had never expected materialized. It isn't often that a person has two major reunions in their lifetime. To help you understand more about Ann's journey, I think it's worth telling you the story of her brother Bill.

CHAPTER 3

BILL

BEFORE MY GRANDPARENTS, James and Cecile, married in 1940, James was embroiled in scandal when he fathered a son as a teenager. In the early 1900s his father, James Edward Sullivan, married his second wife, Sallie. Their union created a blended family in which their children, five each from previous relationships, became step siblings. At 16 years old, James took a liking to his step sister Grace, also 16, despite the taboo that they were technically brother and sister. Before long, young Grace was pregnant with James' baby. Siblings were not supposed to be lovers, so the family had a troubling situation to sort out. They decided it was best to send James Arthur to college at Hampton, as planned, separating the teenage lovers.

Bill Owens, son of James and Grace, was born on October 31, 1931 eleven years before Adeline. Sadly, he had a very unhappy childhood. Grace was very young to be a mother, and the entire situation was sensitive and complicated. Somehow, the family wisdom prescribed that Bill should be raised as Grace's younger brother, not as her son; the adults planned on concealing his mother's identity indefinitely. Everyone maintained the facade for a while, until Sallie told Grace she needed to reveal Bill's relation to her. Bill was 9 years old when he learned that his older sister was really his mother. Even though the secret was out, Bill's conception had been such a disgrace within the family that he was unfairly ostracized for his presence in the world. His own birth was a situation he had not created, but one he would pay the price for and struggle to recover from for the rest of his life.

After James Arthur graduated Hampton and moved his family to Maryland, young Bill, barely acquainted with his father, completely lost touch with him. Bill was raised back in Kentucky with his grandmother Sallie. Grace, who wasn't given the opportunity to attend college, moved to Chicago with her sister, Willy Lee. In her absence, Sallie frequently reminded Bill of his unfavorable status in the family, never letting the pain of his situation fade. She mistreated her grandson so badly that Bill started running away from home. The first few times he fled, he was forced to return to Sallie's unwelcoming home because he was hungry and hadn't planned where he was going. But when Bill made his final run at the age of 14, Sallie made sure to taunt him before he left. "You'll be back here when you get hungry," she declared mockingly. Bill was determined to prove his grandmother wrong and make sure he never returned. He made his way from Kentucky to Chicago, IL, determined to survive and hoping to make a life with his mother.

Living with Grace, Bill quickly realized he wasn't fond of her lifestyle in Chicago. She was still a young woman, and she wasn't ready for the responsibility of parenthood that accompanied Bill's arrival in the Windy City. She was tempted by the allure of the big city's social scene and she wanting to hang out and party. Sometimes Bill's aunt, Willy Lee, cared for him in her place—but she was unkind, just like Sallie had been. When Willy Lee gave him meals, she made him sit on the floor to eat and fed him directly from the pan the food was prepared in, denying him the dignity of sitting at the table with his food served on a plate.

Thankfully, some family members cared for Bill with love and respect, trying to protect him from the tyranny of the others. His aunt Anna in Cincinnati was one of his favorites. He liked his uncle William, known to everyone as "Sonny," and he maintained contact with him over the years. Bill's grandfather, James Edward Sullivan, was also dear to him. James Edward tried to protect his grandson as much as he could, but it wasn't enough to shield him from the abuse that rained down in his absence. As a black sheep in the family, life was hard on Bill. He developed a negative image of his father, who had abandoned him.

Bill knew of his younger sisters, but he had only met Addie twice, once when she was an infant and he was about 12 years old. Recalling her own childhood memories visiting Kentucky, Addie vaguely remembered seeing Bill when she was older. Bill started playing with her on the floor, but one of the adults called him away and they never saw one another again. Bill lived his life knowing his sisters were out there somewhere, always wishing they could have a relationship.

Unfortunately, Bill's life had ramifications for James Arthur's marriage to Cecile. Addie said her mother was notoriously mean to James, and it seemed she never made peace with the fact that he had a son from his brief fling with Grace. Sometimes, when Cecile and James argued, she'd say, "And ya better keep ya thing in ya pants!" This was her most used reference to him having a child who wasn't hers. Bill's existence in the world had unintended consequences that he didn't even realize.

Despite the adversity of his upbringing, Bill capitalized on his intelligence. His mind for everything mechanical made him an excellent tinkerer; he could fix anything. Bill loved jazz music and played upright bass for many years. He had several children from his first marriage: Marla, Bill, and Kelly. While his immediate family was important to him, Bill never talked about his relatives with his children. Marla said, "It was like he didn't have any ancestors."

When Bill met his second wife, Chris, in 1969, she took him to meet her family. He remarked to her that he had never been included in such a happy, positive environment before. Over the years of their marriage, he reminded Chris of her blessings to have lived her wonderful childhood, contrasted with his own. Chris encouraged Bill to have inner strength, release his pain for how he grew up, and to cherish the present and every possibility for their future. She reminded him that the man she married was a strong father, a gifted musician, and very talented with his hands. Chris pointed out that he had a lot to be proud of.

But Bill never saw his own self-worth. The wounds were deep; he harbored resentment and he felt rejected. It was cemented in his mind that sooner or later, everyone would reject him.

Bill was estranged from his father his entire life. He knew James Arthur resided in Maryland, and he really wanted to travel to the east coast to meet the man again one day. Unfortunately, James Arthur's health was deteriorating during the 1970s. A severe blood clot in his leg had affected it so badly, that leg had to be amputated. In 1977, the family considered moving him into a nursing home, where he could receive round-the-clock intensive care. Addie recalled, "I can hear my father's voice now: 'Y'all are *not* putting me in a nursing home!'" In 1978, James fell ill and was hospitalized yet again. One fateful day, when the nurses stepped out of his room to reconcile his medications, James Arthur Sullivan passed away, just two days before being transferred to the nursing home he was desperately avoiding. He died before Bill could ever reconnect with him. Bill didn't learn of his father's passing until after the funeral. The outcast was denied the chance to pay his respects to the father who never openly acknowledged that Bill was his son.

On Labor Day in 2001, Bill's daughter Marla was at her father's house. Glancing at her 70-year-old dad, she noticed his eyes had glazed over. It was clear his mind was off in a distant place. "I hope I can meet my sisters..." he muttered. Marla was astounded. Her father, who had never spoken a word about his family history, had just admitted to her that she had aunts. She was almost 50 years old and for the first time ever, wistful hope for the future had spilled from her father's lips.

Marla immediately recognized the importance of Bill's wish, so she called his wife Chris to recruit her help in finding her father's sisters. Chris knew of Bill's family so she gave Marla the names of a few relatives in Kentucky. Marla eventually tracked down Cecile's home phone number, then called it. She was hoping the phone number was still in service and whoever answered could help her along the journey to connect with Adeline and Ann. Incredibly, Adeline, who was still living in her mother's home after she'd passed away in 1995, answered the phone. Excitedly, Marla identified herself to Addie as her niece, sharing the news that her father wanted to meet his sisters.

Coincidentally, Adeline and Ann had Bill on their minds too. Uncle Sonny, their father's brother, had recently revealed Bill's existence to the sisters, saying, "You know you have a brother out there." The family had kept his existence a secret from the women for decades, but as Sonny's health declined from cancer, he'd reconsidered. He didn't think the truth should go with him to his grave. He felt it was unfair that the siblings had been denied the chance to meet each other for so long.

Marla was so happy to have spoken with Addie, so she quickly called Bill to ask if she could come over to his house. When she arrived, they sat down together, and she looked into her father's eyes. "I contacted your sisters," she said. Bill hadn't had a clue that Marla had taken his quiet wish and worked to make it happen. He was shocked. His eyes widened and he froze like a statue in his seat. Marla told him to pause and take a deep breath before she continued, making sure to underscore that his sisters were excited to hear from him. That night, Bill conference-called Adeline and Ann for an emotional reunion conversation. They took turns trying to acquaint themselves with each other after decades of lost time. They quickly agreed they should make a trip to Kentucky and reunite face to face.

Within two weeks, Bill, a man who had been made to feel inadequate in his family, was finally going home for a long-awaited reunion. Adeline and Ann met their brother for the first time in Mercersburg, KY at Uncle Sonny's home. The trees in the yard were adorned with yellow ribbons commemorating the siblings' long-awaited reunion. Bill was overjoyed to have found his sisters, and they all hugged, cried, and laughed throughout the day with their family. Admiring their brother's features, the women could easily see his resemblance to James Arthur and James Edward, their narrow faces passed down through the generations.

Over the years Ann, Addie, and Bill bonded, but the feelings Bill harbored from his life's experience were too deeply seared into his life to resolve everything with their reunification. Bill was envious of his sisters' upbringing in a two-parent household with his father. When Ann and Adeline reminisced about their childhoods, recounting memories of their father, it upset him. But he was thankful to know and grow to love his sisters in reunion.

Bill Owens had lived a full life estranged from his parents and the rest of his family. His life had been tumultuous; he had lacked a steady foundation, and it's possible that he never fully recovered. Still, he was very thankful for the connection to his sisters. He thanked Marla profusely for finding his family.

Bill Owens died of pancreatic cancer on September 18, 2013, at the age of 82.

CHAPTER 4

VERONICA

IN HER DAY, my mother Veronica was a strong, dedicated, affectionate, loving mother. She raised me as a single mother with my father's support after their divorce in the 1980s. They parented me together, but Mom undeniably did the heavy lifting. When I was sick at night, she was my caregiver. When I had a school project to complete, she gave me encouragement and motivation. She cooked great meals and kept our home spotlessly clean, all while working full time. The daily ups and downs of raising a young man were on her shoulders, and she carried the weight amazingly well.

Mom grew up in a black neighborhood of Kansas City, Missouri. My aunt Bonnie, Veronica's younger sister, shared stories from their youth with me. She described Mom as a homebody and reserved in nature, which were characteristics I also observed. Mom stayed inside the house a lot while the other children were outside playing hide-and-go-seek, which struck Bonnie as strange even then. She was inside with my grandmother Lillie, whom we all called "Momma." When it was too cold to play outside, Momma engaged her four girls—Viola Jeannette (Jean), Rose, Veronica, and Bonnie—in indoor games. Momma challenged them to jacks, pick-up sticks, and checkers, kicking their butts every time.

Who Am I Really?

Momma was a dedicated mother and a deaconess at the church. She always maintained a positive persona for her daughters. She never consumed alcohol, and she tried hiding her cigarette smoking habit from her children as best as she could. She ran the house for the family, stressing out from time to time at the challenges of having a house full of girls.

My grandfather, Randolph Anderson, whom we all called "Daddy," was a deacon in the church and a choir singer with a rich, deep voice. It's rumored that he was a singer for George Washington Carver's peanut commercials on the radio, and was said to have performed before President Roosevelt. When he retired from Prat & Whitney, he started a refrigerator repair business. At the end of each hard day's work, Daddy relaxed at home with a beer and a cigar.

One night at home when the girls were nearly grown, Daddy shared just a little of his alcohol with them, and soon they were feeling tipsy. Veronica decided she wanted to call a young man she had fallen in love with, named Willie. "I love youuu, Willieeee," she wailed and gushed into the phone after drunk dialing her boyfriend. Alcohol consumption, as it so often does, had released the valve holding back her emotions; they flowed out loud for everyone to hear. The alcohol also destroyed Veronica's sense of balance, and she toppled helplessly to the ground. She was literally falling head over heels in love with Willie.

In the 1960's, Veronica worked at the Social Security Administration office in Kansas City, Missouri. That was where she'd met Willie. He was a sharply dressed, intelligent, magnetic guy, and she loved it. The couple were married on October 23, 1966. His career aspirations and the growing array of business opportunities in the Washington, D.C. area drove the couple's migration east, where they settled in a newly-planned community called Columbia, Maryland.

By the early 1970's, Veronica and Willie had been married for several years but weren't getting pregnant. They decided their best option for starting a family was to adopt a child. With the guidance of

Baltimore City Social Services, they completed the adoption application, interviewed with the social worker, and were quickly matched with me. On their way home from picking me up, they stopped at their friends Knowlton and Rosalyn's house. They were also transplants from Kansas City living in Columbia, and Rosalyn was pregnant with their son. Dad put me on the floor to let me crawl around a bit, beaming with pride. "Look at him go! Look at him! That's my son!" he exclaimed.

Dad worked a lot, traveling plenty, and maintained a vibrant social life, even as a new father. He was a young entrepreneur striving to build a business with his partners. The gregarious young entrepreneur was enjoying his success and having fun. Simultaneously, life at home was a strain for Willie. Veronica, who wasn't nearly as outgoing as her husband, began to stress him out. She was changing; situations between them that should have been small issues grew into unnecessarily complex, emotionally-charged problems. Mom and Dad divorced after more than a decade of marriage.

Honestly, I don't even remember my father moving out of our home. I don't recall any huge emotional discussion when my parents told me the family was going to be different, either. Things just gradually changed. He was at home less and less, but it was hard for me to differentiate his business travel from his social gallivanting and general avoidance of his deteriorating marriage. When their relationship was finally over, Dad left most of the furniture at home for us. So, there wasn't any big moving day, no moving truck in our driveway, and no time when half of our home was suddenly empty. By the time they separated, it wasn't that drastic a change for me. At least, I didn't think so.

Veronica was a diligent, hard-working mother, and she relied on the village around us to help her raise her boy. She always maintained close contact with strong female teachers in my schools. On one occasion in elementary school, I was sent to the principal's office for throwing a paper airplane during class, then punching the girl who ratted me out to our teacher. (I gave her a black eye; yes, I know now she was probably my first crush.) The school's principal, Mrs. Betty King, who was also an African-American woman, called my mother to discuss the best course of action in the matter, and Mom granted her permission to punish me accordingly. When she hung up the phone, Mrs. King asked me for the belt from my own pants and proceeded to spank me with it, which Mom would have done herself, if she'd been there.

But Mom couldn't rely on the village for everything. Being present at home with your child is not a task that any parent can assign to a proxy, and mom was dedicated to being with me. It took a major blizzard in the Mid-Atlantic region when I was a kid to help me understand her dedication to making sure I was safe. The afternoon of the impending epic snow storm, the skies darkened as the setting sun was blocked out by the dense clouds and thickly falling snow. I was a latchkey kid growing up, so I was used to being home alone every afternoon after school. This time, she'd called to say she was on her way home before she left the office, so I was more acutely aware that her commute was taking much longer than usual. The mix of heavy snow and thick rush hour traffic heading north from Washington, D.C. was a treacherous combination, and Mom was trapped in it. When she finally reached our home, the snow was so deep in the driveway that she couldn't get her car close to the house. She left her big black Ford Thunderbird stuck in the middle of our cul-de-sac, blocked from advancing by the mound of snow it had plowed to get that far. She shoved the driver's side door open and struggled on foot through the deep snow to our front door. I was watching for her through the window, so I met her at the door. Her tired body practically poured into the foyer, she was so physically and mentally exhausted from the harrowing drive. She seemed deliriously relieved to have made it home, where she collapsed to the floor nearly in tears. The commute that normally took 25 minutes took more than 2 hours that evening; Mom told me that she wasn't sure she would make it home. She was genuinely worried most of the time she'd been alone in her car, so crossing the threshold of our front door was like crawling across the finish line of a grueling event, for which the only reward was to arrive safely at her own home.

Of course, one could argue that Mom had no choice and she had to fight her way home to me. But I've realized, as an adult with children of my own, that much of the hard work and most of the sacrifices we make as parents are lost on our children—at least until they're old enough to reflect. Sometimes a defining event in a child's life underscores their parent's dedication to them. That blizzard was the moment when I watched my mother literally fight the elements of nature to get home to me.

***

Back in Kansas City, Momma was getting older. Her ability to take care of herself had noticeably diminished. At first, Bonnie moved her mother into her own home, where she could keep a closer eye on her. But that closer proximity also helped Bonnie see the stark signs of her mother's dementia, and it worried her. When Momma suffered a fall at Bonnie's house, she realized her mother needed the professional, round-the-clock care of a nursing home.

Mom and I went to visit Momma in that facility when I was a pre-teen. It was hard for my Mom to see her own mother's deterioration, and I felt her anguish. This wonderful lady who used to buzz around her house and navigate her kitchen making meals was confined to a small room with little more than a bed and a window, totally dependent upon the staff, who had many other patients to look after. In the middle of our visit, Momma sat up in her bed and declared it was time for her to get going. When Bonnie asked where she was headed, Momma said, "I need to get to the grocery store, because I have to cook dinner for Randolph." Daddy had been deceased over 15 years at that point. That was my first close encounter with someone with diminished mental function, but there would be more to come.

Who Am I Really?

In May 2001, Momma died. In the weeks after her funeral, Mom told me she felt Momma's presence at our home in Maryland. She said she knew her mother had been in our home, and specifically in her bedroom while she slept; when she woke up, she had detected a very specific smell that reminded her of her youth. I wasn't sure what to think of Mom's ghost story. On one hand, I liked the idea that Mom's mother had paid her a visit from the afterlife to communicate that she was OK. On the other hand, I didn't believe in ghosts. I pondered whether a person's brain could so intensely wish to reminisce on happier days that it could conjure up fond memories subconsciously. I was torn between supporting Mom in her grief and chuckling behind her back at the ridiculous notion that my grandmother's ghost had visited her. But I didn't dare challenge something Mom firmly believed had happened, especially if it meant my grandmother might haunt me for not believing!

Mom retired from State Farm Insurance Company in the early 2000's. At the end of her career, she had become increasingly curmudgeonly, and was often highly irritated with her colleagues. She said her co-workers were getting on her nerves, and told paranoid stories of them talking behind her back. She wasn't enjoying work anymore; she was just executing the job, and it was probably time to move into a new phase of her life. I believed she made the right move and it was time for her to retire.

However, she didn't have a plan for how she intended to spend her abundant free time in retirement. Mom had never remarried after divorcing Dad, and she hadn't dated anyone for years; so, when she retired, she didn't have a life companion to have adventure with. She never had a very large network of close friends, so her social interactions were very limited, when they happened at all. She wasn't involved with any social clubs for seniors, and really didn't have any hobbies that could occupy her time. When she lived in Kansas City, Mom attended church services weekly with her family. But she didn't take me to church as a child in Maryland and hadn't expressed any interest in joining a church for a long time, even for the social fulfillment or spiritual enrichment.

I tried to talk with Mom and help her make plans, but our conversations never yielded meaningful next steps. When she walked out of the State Farm office for the very last time, she walked into one of the worst scenarios possible for a retiree: She went home to be alone.

I believe Mom's solitude, the absence of a daily routine, and lack of interaction with other adults allowed the mental illness festering within her to build strength. However, upon reflection, mental illness had likely taken hold well before she retired. While she was still employed, she complained about the sneaky, conniving behavior of some of her colleagues. I found it odd that they had turned on her, because they were people she'd considered friends for many years. Those complaints of imagined slights by others were some of the first clues of what was to come.

Mom would call me from time to time from home, mostly to ask if I had seen a certain news story on TV that concerned her. I always knew when the phone rang at an odd hour that some special news report had piqued her interest, and she wanted to discuss it.

In the years before her retirement, Mom and I got along very well. We laughed together about a lot of different things, and she proudly watched as I grew into a man. We'd never had an argumentative relationship before, and we had certainly never made one another truly angry. Not too far into her retirement, however, we began to bicker and disagree regularly. We usually argued over what I thought were stupid things, too. The more we spoke to one another, the more we disagreed. Soon, she began to accuse me of saying things that disrespected her—things I never said.

Periodically, she reported that she thought people were following her in her vehicle. One time when I called, she told me there were men in a black car sitting outside and associated their presence directly with my call. She thought I'd hired them. On other occasions, she imagined smells in her apartment. Sometimes, she wondered if those who were following her were trying to poison her. I wondered if the hallucinated smells she experienced then were the same imaginary odors she had detected when her mother's ghost visited us years before. It was all very confusing; nothing was making any sense.

The arguments created deep fractures in our relationship, so it was just easier to speak to her less frequently. I'm not one to face that kind of undue stress. I guess I figured if we were barely talking, I couldn't be accused of disrespecting her. But even after long periods of silence, she still spat venomous accusations of my disrespect into the phone when we talked. She was imagining all of it.

I vividly remember one afternoon when I called her from my car, during the evening commute from Baltimore. There had been a long break since we'd last spoken to one another, so I decided to check in. When she answered the phone, her voice sounded odd: tired, or like she had just completed a big afternoon yawn and stretch. I asked if she had been napping, and kindly apologized if I had woken her. "I am not just laying around here sleeping, Damon!" she hissed in reply. She shouted that she had been doing plenty of things at home, she wasn't just sitting around doing nothing all day, and she didn't appreciate how disrespectful I was being.

That exchange flipped the switch, and I lost control. I usually bite my tongue, especially when engaging with my own mother, but I had *had* it with her challenging my respect for her without reason. I spat back fiercely, defending myself: "I have done nothing *but* respect you! You wanna know what disrespect feels like? I'll show you some f**king disrespect!" I hung up and fumed the rest of the way home, ranting to myself out loud, reliving the conversation. I had never spoken to her like that before. I was all mixed up inside: I was hurt that she thought I would disrespect her, I was angry for how she spoke to me, and I was ashamed for the way I shot back at her with rage. Finally, I was sad that our relationship had deteriorated so badly that ugly arguments were a regular occurrence. When I thought about all that we had been through during that dark time, it cemented in my mind that something was seriously wrong with her. I realized Mom's hallucinations, accusations, and constant general irritation were part of something mentally awry. I needed to take time and think about what to do.

I knew our recent battles had painted me in a bad light, and there was no way I would be able to bring a resolution to our situation alone. It was going to take my commitment, Mom's involvement, and the support of others to get us through this. I called her sister Bonnie, sharing the recent stories of our relationship going completely off the rails. Bonnie reminded me of other instances of mental illness in the family. While it was disappointing to hear that Mom's fate seemed genetically sealed, it was a relief to understand that our antagonistic exchanges were not her choice; her thoughts and actions were beyond her control. Internalizing this allowed me to see Mom through a different lens, giving me a renewed sense of self control in the face of her accusatory outbursts. I had to face the new reality that the loving, nurturing mother I grew up with was fading into the background; a new person I didn't know was in the lead role of Veronica. Keeping that in the front of my mind allowed me to handle our interactions very differently.

It occurred to me that I needed to invite a third party to help us navigate our situation. Third-party conflict mediation was a tactic Mom was familiar with from working in the insurance industry. Court proceedings were time-consuming and expensive endeavors, so the insurance industry often uses mediators to settle disputes between opposing parties outside of court. I figured a counselor serving in that mediator role between us was a plan she could identify with.

So, I tried to get her to see a therapist with me. Michele and I took two of our children to therapy after their adoptions to help them adjust to their new lives in the U.S. and in our home. We also participated in joint therapy sessions during the transition to make sure we were growing into our roles as parents while trying to understand their needs. I told Veronica I would pay for our sessions and offered her the option of helping me find someone for us to see together. I pointed out that we had not made any progress in our conflict resolution efforts alone, and it would help to have another person's perspective. Mom flat-out refused to participate, saying, "Damon, therapy is for white people." I was astonished to hear that comment from her, but with my newly-adopted approach of listening to her with the knowledge that she was not herself anymore, I was able to bite my tongue, not engage in a debate over the merits and benefits of therapy and keep a positive outlook that we could find a path forward together. However, I also realized she was probably expressing deep-seated feelings from her youth. In the African-American community, especially for her generation and those that preceded hers, therapy was not a popular option for resolving anything. You didn't go to therapy, because then someone else would know your business. Pride and privacy were valued more highly than seeking help in the pursuit of personal growth. I closed the door on therapy and began strategizing who an alternative intermediary might be.

Who else could Mom trust? I wondered if I even needed to be involved in her therapy. I thought perhaps I could get a trusted third party to facilitate an intervention with her. I decided to try to speak to her doctor, but I had no idea who her doctor was. I would have to trick Veronica into telling me.

Several weeks later, I got Mom on the phone again. We exchanged some high-level pleasantries, then I asked about her diet and exercise, topics she always liked to talk about. She frequently tried new recipes and seemed to be on and off diets my whole life. I needed to appear to be genuinely concerned, but also be on the path to getting her doctor's name. When she told me her health status, I saw my opening. I asked, "What does your doctor think of your progress?" Her doctor was proud of her. "That's great," I said carefully, "I know you really like your current doctor. What's her name again?" I had tricked her into identifying her primary care physician. I repeated the name over and over in my head for the rest of the conversation. I had to remember that name.

Within a few days, I had made an appointment to speak with Mom's physician by phone. I knew she would be very cautious about speaking with her patient's family members without the patient's consent, so I started right there. I told the doctor, "I know you can't give me any information about my mother due to privacy protection laws and doctor-patient privilege. So I'm just going to talk, and I'd like you to listen, please." I began by telling the doctor that if Mom knew I had called her, she would be furious. It could be the end of our relationship if she found out, and I admitted I was desperate. I explained the entirety of the situation and detailed all the erratic behavior and hallucinations. I implored her for help, explained the failed attempt to get Veronica into joint therapy, and reminded the doctor again how disastrous it could be if Mom knew that we had spoken. I stressed that I needed her assistance. The doctor thanked me for calling, said she'd see what she could do, and we hung up.

I immediately felt better. This tactic had to work. Mom wouldn't trust anyone more than her own doctor, and I made it clear our clandestine call had to remain a secret. I felt we were on the path to healing, and I breathed a sigh of relief.

A week later, Mom called me. She had found out that I had spoken with her doctor, and she *was* absolutely furious My heart sank lower than it ever had before. "How could you do this to me, Damon?" she asked. She felt betrayed and couldn't understand how I could behave that way, going against my own mother. Either Mom read her own chart in the doctor's office, or the doctor or her staff had told Mom I called. The same way Mom was furious with me, I was furious with the doctor's office. I wrote them a scathing letter explaining the entire situation and the damage that had ultimately been done, while I was desperately trying to get my mother some help. I never heard a reply from the doctor's office.

Who Am I Really?

The chasm between Veronica and I kept growing deeper and wider, and I didn't know how to stop it.

At first, mental illness can be an elusive specter to detect, when you're not familiar with what to look for. Loved ones and friends close to a person who is deteriorating don't necessarily receive overt signals that something is going wrong, like we do in other aspects of our lives. There's no warning light that starts to flash like when your vehicle needs maintenance. It's not like sports, where broken rules and fouls are signaled obviously with whistles and flags. There's no sign on the side of the road of life that warns you of dangerous sharp turns ahead. Mental illness was operating behind the scenes until the day I realized that what I was experiencing with Mom wasn't just weird, uncharacteristic behavior in our relationship; she had a real, undiagnosed problem, and it was the tragic star of the show from then on.

That was a very hard time for us both, and it continues to be difficult for us to this day. For me, my trusted parent—who dutifully took me to soccer practice and was in frequent contact with my teachers about my progress because she cared about my success—was living in an alternate reality from my own. She thought people were spying on her with listening devices, was sure the air in her home was being poisoned through the ventilation system, and insisted I was a disrespectful son.

For years, Veronica told me she wanted to move back to Missouri to be near her family. It had been decades since she had lived near her sisters, so I understood the magnetic pull to move closer to her roots. Still, somehow her casual hints at relocating always sounded aspirational, lacking commitment.

One January day, after another drought of no contact with Mom, I received a birthday card in the mail from her, addressed to my son Seth. It was nice that she remembered his birthday, and for a moment, I smiled. My heart was warmed by her thoughtfulness. Then I noticed something strange in the upper left corner of the envelope. A return address sticker was there, and her name was on it, but the address was an unfamiliar place in Raymore, Missouri. "I'll be damned, she moved!" I said in disbelief, yet with full acknowledgement of a new reality at the same time. She had moved away without saying a word, only meeting her grandson once. I felt sorry for her, that she was no longer capable of sharing something as momentous as a move to the Midwest with me, and sad that I was losing the mother I once knew. But mental illness isn't some amazing, reliable best friend, and it wasn't nearly as thoughtful as I would have liked it to be with my feelings.

Veronica had bought a single-family home in Raymore. She settled into a new life and new routines amidst the clouds swirling around in her mind. Bonnie, a talented beautician who lives in the area, told me that Veronica frequented her hair salon to have her hair cut by her sister. Things seemed to be OK between them, but Bonnie never forgot our conversations about how Veronica's mental health was deteriorating. During their salon visits and in phone conversations, Bonnie tried to convince Veronica to finally reveal to me that she had moved away. She had been in Missouri for months before sending that birthday card to Seth, revealing the truth.

Bonnie told me that one day, Veronica very seriously said, "Bonnie, they've followed me here," referring to the imaginary stalkers who had terrorized her in Maryland. Bonnie was witnessing first-hand the state of her sister's brain.

Months later, Veronica had an episode that finally forced a diagnosis. She had packed a suitcase and a random assortment of household items in the back of her silver Lexus, then drove two hours from her home in Raymore to Columbia, Missouri (a city with, perhaps coincidentally, the same name as my childhood hometown, but in her new home state). She parked her car in a random family's driveway, in an undesirable neighborhood. Veronica began knocking on doors, telling anyone who answered that she was looking for her boyfriend's home. But she didn't have a boyfriend.

Who Am I Really?

When the police arrived, they asked Veronica if there was anyone they could call on her behalf, and she named Bonnie. Speaking with the police officer, Bonnie emphatically told him that Veronica desperately needed help, and she pleaded with him to deliver Veronica to a mental institution. The officer replied that he could assist Veronica to get help, but he would have to recommend a psychological evaluation to the staff at the local hospital. The University Hospital of Columbia agreed she needed mental health assistance, and she was committed for 10 days.

On her first visit, Bonnie was heartbroken to find her sister in ankle cuffs. My mother was considered a flight risk, so they had shackled her to protect her from herself. I spoke with Mom by phone soon after the facility stabilized her with medication. She reassured me that she was OK, explaining that she'd had an episode when she had gotten very confused. She sounded good to me, creating a wave of gratitude within me that she was finally beginning her recovery. But I remained vigilant, preparing myself for the rip current that could sweep her away again after she left that place.

Veronica was released from the institution under her own recognizance, and prescribed more medication to help her manage her mental state from home. Sure enough, as is often the case with patients of any kind, the medicine made her feel much better—so she decided she no longer needed it. It's a vicious circle with so many people: wanting to feel better, not wanting to be on meds, stopping the meds, feeling poorly again—but not wanting to take those same meds to feel better again. To date, Mom hasn't had another episode of the magnitude that got her institutionalized, but our family lives with the ongoing concern that one day, we'll receive another call from another police officer. Until then, there's nothing we can do. We cannot intervene on Veronica's behalf until she proves she's a danger to herself or to others.

CHAPTER 5

WILLIE

E VERYONE WHO EVER met my father, Willie Davis, said he was one of a kind—and they were spot on. Honestly, it was hard to be unhappy around my dad. He just wouldn't let it happen. He wanted you to enjoy life with him and feel strength within yourself; he empowered you to feel like you could accomplish amazing things. If you were down, he would talk to you about whatever was challenging you, offer his opinion to help you gain some perspective, and then say something to rebuild your strength. Then, he would lighten the mood with a silly or obnoxious comment designed to make you laugh. He had an incredible spirit that connected with people of all ages, all ethnicities, and every socio-economic background. Dad had a big heart and a generous spirit.

Born in 1942 in Tallulah, Mississippi, Dad grew up in Kansas City, Kansas during the era of racial segregation. Kansas was a "free state," but Jim Crow segregation persisted in their community. Willie's lifelong friend, Waymon Guinn, described the black community where they grew up as having segregated schools and black-owned businesses on every corner. Waymon and Willie met in their early teen years at junior high school. They lived in the North End area of the city, between 3rd and 10th streets, and became close buddies in high school.

Who Am I Really?

In their neighborhood, boys got themselves into social clubs, not gangs. The "Vireos" who came from the 5th street area, were usually athletes, and were known to be rebel rousers. The "Frocks" recruited kids from all over, and were usually studious guys. Waymon said he and Willie were "Flamingos." When I heard the name of their social club, I had to admit it matched Dad's persona. As an adult, he was always well dressed and well groomed, or "clean," as they used to say in the black community. The Flamingos also came from all over, and were generally the slicker, more streetwise, well-dressed crew of the three. Even if their clothes weren't the most expensive threads, they knew how to put their outfits together with style. The Flamingos even wore suits to high school one day a week. When then Vireos challenged their style and began wearing suits to school too, the Flamingos upped their game to wearing suits one week a month, carrying briefcases for emphasis.

A lot of their time as teens was spent in the streets and the pool halls of the area. But Dad's crew were some cool cats, avoiding conflicts and focusing on the smoother side of life. They hosted regular socials, where each guy would have the other fellas over for a meeting. They listened to jazz, talked about everything under the sun, and shared food. Waymon said Dad loved to bake, so when it was his turn to host, often he had made a cake or some other baked treat.

Astonishingly, Waymon painted Willie as a quiet guy in high school. Back then, his personality was overshadowed by his older brother Eddie. "The Willie Davis that you knew," Waymon said, "was the exact opposite when he was growing up. He was very cool, but you wouldn't even know he was in the room." I was incredulous when I heard that portrayal of Dad; the man I knew was usually one of the most gregarious, boisterous people wherever we went.

Willie was raised by his grandmother, Dellar Hamblet, whom the family simply called "Momma Della." Dad held Momma Della in the highest regard for all she did to mold him into a man. He called her his "rock." In one Facebook post, he said: "She shaped me ethically, spiritually, and inspired me with kindness to all." One of the pictures he held most dear was a portrait of himself in his Air Force uniform, with Momma Della painted in next to him.

Dad was a studious guy at Northeast High School. The school was in the heart of the black neighborhood, and it was filled with African-American teachers who held advanced degrees in their courses of study. They pushed the children's education as best they could, with the limited resources allotted to them. When Dad graduated high school, he attended junior college. His studious nature persisted into adulthood, and I saw it in him when I was a kid. He frequently went to the local library to soak up knowledge and satisfy his curiosities.

Dad once told me that even when he was a young man, he knew he wanted to escape Kansas City to see the rest of the world. The opportunity to expand his horizons was granted when he enlisted in the U.S. Air Force (USAF). He joined the military to take advantage of the G.I. Bill: government educational and other assistance to military veterans, in exchange for military service. He served as a Medical Administrative Specialist, Private First Class and raved about the Air Force to Waymon and their friends. Persuaded by Willie's salesmanship, Waymon joined the Air Force too. Coincidentally, he was assigned to the same specialist position as Dad, but in a different unit. During his four years with the Air Force, Dad's duty stations took him to March Air Force Base in California and Ramey Air Force Base in Puerto Rico. His travels opened his eyes to the world of opportunities outside of Kansas City, and created a deeper thirst for exploration and social adventure.

When his military service was fulfilled, Willie returned to Kansas City and accepted an entry-level position with the Social Security Administration. In government, the General Schedule (GS) is a pay scale for employees in civil service. Dad's job only landed him a GS-1, the lowest level on the GS scale—and well beneath his true qualifications, after years of junior college and military service. Good jobs were in short supply for men and women of African-American descent during that era, regardless of their training. Still, employment meant a paycheck, and that meant he had purchasing power.

Willie continued to dress for success the way he had as a young Flamingo. He bought nice clothes and shoes, and even set his sights on owning a car. With no driver's license and no clue how to operate a motor vehicle, Willie bought a 1967 Chevrolet Impala, one of the coolest cars on the road at the time. Since he couldn't drive, he asked a friend to drive it home from the dealership.

Material items often caught Willie's eye, but so did a young woman who also worked at the Social Security office. Veronica Anderson was a beautiful, light-skinned woman Willie had fallen for quickly, and soon they were busy planning a wedding.

Dad attended Rockhurst University and worked part-time at Ford Motor Company for a while. Then, he earned his Master of Business Administration (MBA) from University of Massachusetts Amherst. When he returned to Kansas City, he started working for the Black Economic Union, a predecessor to many of the economic development organizations still operating in the city today.

Dad was still in touch with his contemporaries at UMASS, and many of them touted the job opportunities in federal government contracting in the Washington, D.C. area. Willie recognized the chance for career advancement, so he and Veronica relocated to Maryland, opening a new chapter in their lives together. He worked with Macro Systems for several years, forming relationships across the country. Dad bonded with several of his colleagues at Macro, especially one of the company vice presidents, Herb Birch. Dad, Herb, Waymon and several other guys from Kansas City worked hard and played hard together. They eventually decided to team up and launch their own consulting firm. It was through their friendship that Birch & Davis Associates, Inc. was born.

It wasn't until I was a young adult that I realized my Dad used to spend his money fairly extravagantly. He always bought the latest

Cadillac Seville when I was a kid. When he switched his automobile brand loyalty, he got the hottest little red Mercedes-Benz 500SL around. His image, and other people's perception of him, meant a lot to Dad—including my image of him. Of course, I loved him no matter what, but his absence from my daily life as a child seemed to bring him some guilt. On one birthday when I was about 10 years old, I simply wanted a small, battery-powered piano keyboard that I could put on my lap and play. In my mind, I was just trying to feel out whether I was into music at all. When my birthday was approaching, mom told him I was exploring music. But Dad's tastes were large and flashy; on that birthday, I got a huge piano keyboard on a stand the size a professional musician might use for a paid gig. There I was, barely interested in music and had never taken a piano lesson, with a massive, intimidating instrument presented to me. I rarely touched it. If it hadn't been for the pre-programmed demo song you could listen to with the touch of one button, it never would have played a full song in its life.

Everywhere I went with my Dad, he knew someone there. One year, we stopped at a Christmas tree lot on Georgia Avenue in Silver Spring, MD. After we picked out our tree, Dad paused and looked at the tree salesman sitting on the other side of the campfire. He called out, "Hey, I know you!" They soon figured out they had been drinking at a local bar together in the months prior. On another occasion, when I was about 15 years old, we were on the Caribbean island of Saint Maarten for vacation. As we had been many times before, we were at a local bar. As the evening crept on, Dad recognized his duty to be a responsible parent, deciding he shouldn't keep his son out too late; he knew Veronica wouldn't approve. We decided to go back to our hotel for the night, but as we drove along the winding island roads, we second guessed our impulse to be so responsible in the absence of authority (Mom). Dad looked at me and asked, "Why are we going home so early? We don't have a single thing to do tomorrow!" He was right; we had nothing scheduled and no responsibilities the next morning. We made a U-turn and headed right back to the bar, where—lo and behold—Dad recognized an acquaintance from the D.C. area.

If he didn't already know someone wherever he was, Dad would make sure to introduce himself to a variety of people. He had a magnetism that was undeniable. He was well-traveled; therefore, he could talk to almost anyone about places he had been, or one of his experiences similar to theirs. One of his sisters, my aunt Shirley, once said, "D never met a stranger," lovingly referring to him by his last initial. I hope you're thinking *I didn't even know this guy, but I really like him.* Willie Davis was one of those once-in-a-lifetime people you were happy was in your world.

CHAPTER 6

Damon—Columbia, MD

IN 1967, THE ROUSE COMPANY opened the planned community of "Columbia" in Howard County, Maryland. The county was mostly farmland when Rouse launched its ambitious and visionary development plans. Strategically located 20 miles south of Baltimore and 30 miles north of Washington, D.C., it offered bedroom community sanctuary from its urban neighbors. Columbia was built to "eliminate racial, religious, and class segregation" through its model of eliminating subdivisions and integrating people of various backgrounds within each neighborhood. The community was broken into 10 villages, where each neighborhood and its streets were creatively named after inspiring and tranquil elements of nature, or the poetry and literary works of Henry Longfellow and J.R.R. Tolkien. One area is called Hobbit's Glen. The village I lived in was Hickory Ridge, the namesake of a nearby 1700s slave plantation. Our home was on "Bright Plume," and my friends lived on other cleverly named streets: Sunny Spring, Cricket Pass, Golden Hook, and Slender Sky. We were a middle-class family in a city where people of various racial backgrounds from differing socioeconomic strata were intentionally integrated. In 1970, the population was roughly 9,000 people. Today, Columbia is home to 99,000 people. In 2016, it was ranked #1 on *Money* magazine's list of "Best Places to Live."

Who Am I Really?

When we first moved to Hickory Ridge, I was about seven years old. As I grew older, I played outside all over my neighborhood. I cleared sticks and leaves that jammed the creeks. We played football and soccer on the neighborhood fields and I was in and out of my friends' houses. I could go anywhere I wanted on my bike, using the network of winding paved trails through the wooded areas. It was a great little utopia for young families to raise children. My best friend Scott Habicht was white, and we were always together. When we were teenagers, Scott's mom recounted the first time he and I met each other. She said Scott reached out with curiosity and gently touched my tightly curled brownish-red Afro with his little hands. On some level, we knew we were different from one another, but our differences didn't matter. They rarely do, with young children. We were two boys of the same age living across the street from one another, and that was all that was important. Interracial friendships like ours grew by the thousands like beautiful wildflowers all over Columbia as the city's population grew.

I had a fun, enriching childhood in Columbia. Every summer I spent my time in day camps, playing sports in the sun, swimming in the pool, and playing flashlight tag in the neighborhood at night. As the long hot summers unfolded, my mom occasionally commented on the hues of reddish brown in my hair that seemed to get brighter red with more exposure to the bright sunlight. I didn't think twice about my hair color over the years, cutting it shorter every year, until I maintained a bald head after college. But decades later, her voice commenting on my reddish Afro would ring in my head again.

In adolescence, I started to notice more clearly how different each family was from another across the community. Some of my peers' parents were married for many years, while other kids had stepmothers, stepfathers, and step siblings. In some families, the children bore striking resemblances to their parents and siblings, while other kids didn't look like their parents at all, to me. I saw Caucasian mothers with brown or Asian children and just assumed those kids were adopted, like me. (It never occurred to me at the time that they could be the offspring of interracial couples.) I wondered what it was like for those adoptees to live in a house where they didn't look like their parents or siblings, and I appreciated my resemblance to my family.

Mom and Dad divorced when I was about 12 years old. I was attending Harper's Choice Middle School at the time, where the requirement to be more responsible for my school work was a challenge for me. I was never a very good student; I lacked the burning sense of responsibility to get my homework done. My motivation to do my work was mostly the fear of disappointing my parents with my poor performance. But the biggest issue for me during that time of my life was that change in our family.

My grades slipped precipitously the year Dad moved out. Mom, who had always been the disciplinarian and the one to lend structure to our home, was by default the schoolwork taskmaster. At the end of one marking period, my English teacher revealed her grade book to Mom and me during parent teacher conferences. We sat across the table from my teacher as she pointed to the row with my name on the left. As her pen scrolled across the page, she highlighted how column after column had blank boxes where I should have earned grades for my work. Mom had witnessed me completing the assignments every night, so she knew the work had been done. Therefore, she was baffled by the mystery of where the completed assignments had gone, disappearing between home and the classroom. We went to my locker to investigate, and sure enough, nearly every single assignment was haphazardly stuffed inside, mingled with a pile of stinky gym clothes and miscellaneous garbage. We stood in the hallway together cleaning out my locker, unfolding and smoothing page after page of missing assignments, my grades jumping up by a few points with each one. The adults concluded the divorce had affected me in some weird way, but I just felt unorganized.

I had a pretty typical teenage experience in Columbia. Mom worked until 6 p.m. every day, so I was a latchkey kid, starting in middle school.

Who Am I Really?

I was trusted with the responsibility to let myself in the house and behave appropriately while unsupervised. Every afternoon I was at home alone, completing my homework, then sitting in front of the television watching cartoons with a huge bowl of cereal. I was assigned chores too, but of course I never did them until minutes before I knew Mom was due to arrive home from work. Usually, I lay on the couch until I saw her car pulling into the driveway. In a mad dash, I sprinted through the house emptying trash cans, feverishly closing the blinds, or recklessly emptying the dishwasher. It was just the two of us in our home, so I had to help out with chores for everything to run smoothly. I learned a lot of responsibility for how to take care of a home back then.

I was a late bloomer at Wilde Lake High School, a naïve and immature freshman in a school full of young adults. However, I was lucky because I got along with most people. I played soccer in the fall and lacrosse in the spring, but I was just on the team: not a great athlete. Still, being a high school athlete meant I was friendly with athletic guys and girls. I also got along with kids who enjoyed other activities, so I had a fairly wide social circle. I traveled with a small crew of guys—Paul Innella, Oba McMillan, Andre McCallum, and the son of one of Dad's good friends, Keith Gonsouland—and we traversed the school's social circles together, trying to stay out of trouble and get in with all the right folks.

My parents were pretty happy with our experience and my upbringing in Columbia, but periodically I sensed their concern about my lack of cultural identity. They both grew up in Midwestern black communities during a racially charged era. In Columbia, my experiences had been interracial or predominantly white, and completely different from theirs. Still, they never interfered in my choices, allowing me to find my own way most of the time.

For example, my Dad played basketball growing up and in the Air Force. I grew up playing soccer and lacrosse, sports he couldn't identify with. I laugh every time I reminisce about the day I called Dad to ask him to buy me lacrosse equipment.

"Lacrosse, what's that!?" he asked with bewilderment.

"Well, it was a Native American sport. You have a stick with a net on the end and you toss the ball to one another and try to score goals. It's a little bit like basketball and ice hockey, but on grass," I tried to explain.

"Isn't that a white boy sport, Damon?" he enquired earnestly.

"Uh… well…" I stammered, unsure how to respond.

He paused for a minute, and I waited, hoping he would say my equipment purchase request was approved. Instead he said jokingly, "I don't know if I like the idea of a bunch of white boys chasing you with sticks!" We burst out laughing, then he agreed to take me to buy my gear. That conversation was a comical exemplar of how different my life had been from theirs.

At about 15 years old, I started sneaking out of Mom's house at night. My friends were allowed to stay out later than I, so I was missing out on good times when I went home to obey my curfew. I didn't bother to ask for a later curfew; I just broke the rules. One day while chatting with Mom, I found the loophole that allowed my repetitive escapes. She admitted to me that she never slept very well while I was out with my friends, and only fell into a much deeper sleep when she knew I was home safe. Being a manipulative teenager, I took advantage of that valuable information. I started making a big production of it when I got home at night. My keys jingled loudly, the door opened forcefully and closed firmly. I made sure to speak loudly enough to be positive I was heard when I announced, "I'm home, Mom." She would reply, "OK, OK," seemingly drifting into deeper sleep as she spoke. Then, I moved quickly to my room upstairs, right next door to hers, and turned on a little music to drown out the noise of my bedroom window opening, and the screen being removed. I turned off the music and said, "Good night, Mom," to signal that I was going to sleep. I waited a minute or two to be sure the coast was clear, then slipped out of my window and closed it carefully behind me. I climbed over the deck railing, which I had reinforced after school with extra nails, then jumped down to the ground. Once down, I raced around to the front of my house, where my buddy Keith was always waiting for me. I had a key to the car that would eventually be mine when I turned 16, so we took it out at night. The last thing I needed was for the sound of my car starting to wake my mother or the neighbors, so we devised an elaborate strategy to sneak the vehicle away undetected. I would quickly jump in the driver's side, roll down the windows, and put the vehicle in neutral. After I climbed back out the window, Keith and I would push the car out of its parking space and roll it down the street, where we hopped in our respective windows. Safely distant, I started the car in neutral and drove off into the night. Having a car gave us access to an entire world of adventures that were well beyond walking distance.

When our late-night antics were over and it was time to go home, I would put the gas pedal to the floor at the entrance to our neighborhood and race my car up Bright Plume at top speed. I threw the car in neutral, turned off the ignition and lights, and battled the powerless steering to get the vehicle back into its parking space. Keith and I would smack hands, say our goodbyes, and he would walk home to sneak into his own house on Cricket Pass. I walked around to the back of mine, jumped up to the deck, and pulled myself up on the two specific pieces I had reinforced. I climbed over the rail and into my window, replaced the screen, and went to sleep. Invariably, the next day I would look outside to see my car had been terribly parked the night before. But Mom never seemed to notice.

What she did notice was her dead plant, right under my window. Weekend after weekend, when jumping off my deck, I was landing on a bush that I had helped her plant. When we went outside to lay mulch or pull weeds, Mom was completely perplexed as to why the bushes on the right and left were alive and well, but the bush in the middle was dead. I had stomped the life out of that poor bush in search of fun.

Columbia was built to integrate cultures and transcend broader, societal biases in the 1960s and '70s. But as I was growing up in the 1980s and '90s, the mainstream media and the rest of the country did not portray the same level of integration. Very few TV shows, news programs, or magazine covers featured people of color.

Of course, an integrated community naturally led to a lot of interracial dating. In high school, many of the black males, athletes and scholars alike, dated white females. They were guys I looked up to, so my friends and I followed suit. Conversely, there were plenty of white guys who were dating black females. Columbia, Maryland has been known to produce a lot of interracial couples and lots of beautiful mixed-raced children over the years. It was how we were raised.

My homecoming and prom dates were almost always white women, save one Asian. My senior year was the same as the prior years, except my prom date's parents didn't know that her date was black. While they lived in Columbia and presumably appreciated all that the city stood for, it's unlikely that they fully subscribed to the myriad of ways an interracial community might impact their family.

Of course, senior prom is a major event in a young woman's life, and there's a lot of pomp and circumstance involved with her date arriving to pick her up. To go to prom with my date, I needed a plan. My buddy Zach Toback, a guy I frequently used as my alibi with Mom, whether we had been together or not, arranged to be my surrogate in front of her parents. I gave Zach the corsage I had gotten her. He went to her house, placed the corsage on her wrist, and took the obligatory pictures in front of the family, then he left with their daughter, my prom date. Zach brought her to me, waiting around the corner in my car. The whole thing started as a simple charade to get out and have some fun with a popular girl. When I reflected on the whole experience later, I felt embarrassed that I had agreed to hide myself to go on one date. It was sobering and validated the choices I had already made for the next stage of my life, college.

Who Am I Really?

Back in my junior year of high school, I'd had the serious discussion about my college options with my parents. Like millions of other families, we developed a list of universities that seemed to be safe bets for my acceptance, University of Maryland among them. I was very familiar with Maryland's campus, but it was too close to home. Like many teenagers, I wanted a new experience somewhere else. I put Wake Forest on the long-shot list, and saw I needed a few others that were solid choices, where I had a pretty good chance of being accepted. My parents suggested that I might think about attending a historically black college or university (HBCU), and I was receptive to the idea.

While researching other Maryland schools, I learned about an HBCU called University of Maryland Eastern Shore (UMES), and I thought hard about applying to attend. I liked the idea of UMES, but like University of Maryland, it was too close to home—and I hadn't been there for a visit. With maturity, I reflected on how I felt comfortable with my ability to navigate the utopian society Columbia portrayed. It provided a sanitized version of the real world. I wanted to see what it was like to attend a school with students who looked like me and came from communities and neighborhoods that didn't resemble Columbia at all. I knew how to navigate the predominantly white world that I was raised in; I wanted to learn how to navigate the black community, too. The idea of going to an HBCU was growing on me.

My parents arranged for me to go on an HBCU bus tour with a group of high school students. The tour started in Washington, D.C., and traveled for miles, taking us to South Carolina State University (SCSU), North Carolina Agricultural & Technical University (NCA&T), and Hampton University, just to name a few. The schools located in the deeper south didn't appeal to me, but something about Hampton University felt right. The school is located on the water near Newport News, Virginia, where the United States Navy has a base and major shipbuilders have large-scale operations. The campus was serene and beautiful, surrounded on three sides by water; I could instantly see myself as a student there. I applied for admission and was accepted, for the fall semester of 1990. Hampton would be my "home by the sea" for the next four years.

When students arrive on their new college campus, they rarely have a deep knowledge of the amazing things that happened there before they arrived, and I was the same. I had no feel for the eclectic set of attendees and graduates who preceded me at Hampton. The school has a rich history in America, starting with its informal formation in 1861. Hampton was opened to educate freed slaves, many of whom escaped bondage to search for freedom, and found their way to an education. The very first class was taught by a woman named Mary Peake under a small oak tree, which is still alive on campus today. In 1863, that same tree, known as the Emancipation Oak, was the first place in the South where President Abraham Lincoln's Emancipation Proclamation was read, declaring that nearly 3 million formerly-enslaved people were then freed in 10 southern states. Hampton University was formally established in 1868, and has graduated an array of noteworthy individuals like Booker T. Washington, who went on to help found Tuskegee Institute in Alabama; Charles Phillips, former CEO of Oracle; Freeman A. Hrabrowski, III, President of the University of Maryland Baltimore County (UMBC); Wanda Sykes, comedian; Mary Jackson, the pioneering NASA engineer whose story is featured in the book and film adaptation *Hidden Figures*; several amazing NFL and NBA athletes, and even a track and field Olympian, Kellie Wells.[1]

The college tours were an amazing experience, but since they took place over the summer, each campus was devoid of its bustling student body. Our tour guides showed us what an HBCU campus looked like, but without students, we didn't see what HBCU student life would be like. I hadn't done a very good job imagining it, either. I guess my mind defaulted to what I had always known: an integrated student body. On

---

[1] http://www.hamptonu.edu/about/history.cfm

moving day, after three hours of driving from Maryland toward the eastern shore of Virginia, Mom and I arrived on campus, checked in at the requisite stations, and began to unpack our overstuffed little hatchback car. The campus was a buzzing hive of activity. Students, parents, and faculty were walking the streets and streaming in and out of buildings, making the campus come to life. It didn't take very long for it to sink in that every kid in my classes, in the dining hall, or at football and basketball games looked just like me. It was incredible. I rarely thought about people's race much before that first semester, so it was a reality check for nearly every student to be of African descent. Of course, that first culture shock was followed by a second realization I hadn't anticipated.

At the end of the first semester, the school closed for winter break, so it was time to head home. Mom dutifully made the three-hour trek down to HU, picked me up, and we headed back up the highway to Maryland. It was great to see Mom, and I could feel that she was proud of her college man. I'm sure she could see differences in me already, and I know she was excited to have me back at home. Of course, all my friends were returning from their schools too, so we quickly made plans to meet up for the night to hit some of our old haunts. We socialized at the 7-Eleven in Running Brook. There was a small field party on the practice field at Wilde Lake High School. And we popped in and out of one another's houses throughout the break. I figured going home would be just like old times, but I was surprised by my second racial awakening. For the first time, I realized how many of my friends were white. I wasn't disturbed by the revelation; they were still my friends. But that first semester was an eye-opening experience toward racial awareness that I didn't have before. I grew up with such a sense of equality among everyone that race hadn't been a factor in my friendships. Sure, I had some moments when I was frustrated with the families of white girls who wouldn't let me date their daughters. But those moments were fleeting, as the issues of racial tension were explained to me by the girl herself, not in a face-to-face confrontation with her parents, where the discrimination would be a stark reality. I just went back to my circle of friends and we all got along great. But after one semester at an HBCU, I suddenly saw people for the color of their skin more clearly. I had opposing feelings: both an odd sense of gratitude that my eyes were opened, and nostalgia for the ignorant bliss that blindly assumes everyone's equality. There was something very pure about my prior mindset, even if it was an unrealistic existence for the rest of the world to uphold.

In college, I continued my academic mediocrity. I studied for a business degree, but it didn't ignite any passion within me. Studying business was safe. It was a generic major with broad possibilities, covering my bases for a very uncertain future. In my sophomore year, I was failing a few classes and my mother was concerned. She strategically deployed my father to take a trip down to school to meet with me and my professors to get me back on track. She had been very involved with my schoolwork before college, attending every teacher conference and keeping me focused enough to reach college. But Hampton was three hours from Columbia—and it was probably Dad's turn to show some concern for my work, which he was paying for.

The day Dad visited me at school, I had mixed emotions. No one likes being in trouble with their parents, and for him to have to drive three hours to my school meant I was really messing up. But being in trouble with Dad had a nonchalance that was drastically different from the intensity of Mom's stern guidance. When he rolled onto campus in his bright red convertible Cadillac Allante, it was the coolest kind of trouble to be in. My friends on campus were seeing me in his slick car, and I don't even remember any meetings with my professors. My Dad was in town, and it felt great. I got the message that I needed to straighten up my grades, he left me some cash, and then he was gone.

Graduation from Hampton University in the spring of 1994 was a proud moment for me. I was thankful for my college experience and I was grateful to my parents for funding my education. I rarely returned to Hampton's campus, but the school would return to me years later in the most unpredictable way.

I Knew My In-Laws Before I Met My Wife

While I was at Hampton, Willie had reached the end of his second marriage to a woman named Libby. He had found love again with a beautiful younger woman named Hazel. She was more outgoing than Veronica and Libby, and her disposition allowed her to hang with Dad socially. Dad liked having a partner who could roll with his energy.

Hazel was from St. Vincent and the Grenadines (SVG), a small island nation in the Caribbean. It's a volcanic island with rich soil and lush greenery growing abundantly. The island has yet to benefit from a tourism boom like larger West Indian islands, so a trip there is an immersive Caribbean experience. Dad loved to travel and explore local cultures, so St. Vincent was a perfect destination for him. For a few years while they were dating, Dad would come home from St. Vincent and exclaim, "Aw, man, you gotta take a trip down there with me!" He never gave much consideration to the responsibilities you had in your life when he was planning his fun, so I reminded Dad that I was a college student, broke, and busy. But I also recognized that a chance to hang with my father on vacation wasn't to be missed, if there was any way to make it happen. I proposed that he pay for my trip, and soon I would join them in their Caribbean vacations.

Every summer, the Caribbean islands blossom with energy as Carnival festivities ignite celebrations of West Indian heritage. If you haven't seen a Carnival festival in person, it's a massive, unforgettable, party spectacle. Caribbean rhythms constantly thump from a parade of trucks rigged with enormous sound systems. Huge groups of beautifully-costumed masqueraders dance for hours in the hot sun, marching up and down the city streets. Revelers from every walk of life drink and eat every hour of the day, night, and into the morning. Our first few trips to the island were drunken, food-filled escapes from reality. We trekked into downtown late at night, partying and consuming copious amounts of alcohol until the sun came up.

I've never been one to introduce myself to women, and Dad recognized my reserved disposition with the opposite sex. Embarrassingly, he would call out to a young lady he had just met himself, and say, "Come here, I want you to meet my son!" As the social scene flowed around us, Dad struck up conversations with still more new acquaintances, and within minutes, he would introduce the poor girl to them as if we were actually dating: "I want you to meet Damon's girlfriend!" She would invariably blush and smile, and I was totally embarrassed by the antics of one of the best wingmen ever.

Of course, when the parties were done, there was nothing better than unwinding in the sun, swimming in the ocean surf, or just relaxing on the sand, soaking in the slow-paced vibe of the islands.

Dad was adept at immersing himself in local culture, wherever he traveled. He didn't want to go where the tourist traps were. He wanted to meet real, local people, and have authentic local experiences. After many years of visits, the island was starting to feel like a second home. One of his closest friends was a well-known doctor on the island, Sir Fredrick Ballantyne. "Freddy," or "Doc" as he was sometimes called, was a cardiologist, philanthropist, entrepreneur, and somewhat of a local celebrity despite his very low-key demeanor.

Doc loved to sail and fish the seas, and he always made sure his family and friends were along for these trips. On Freddy's boat, I met some of his children, Marcus and Melissa, and several grandchildren. Marcus and I were close in age, so we got along well. In time, I started staying at Marcus' house on our Vincentian vacations. Back then, he had one son, Jamal, and a daughter, Kayla, on the way. Marcus and Melissa had another brother, Carl, whom I only met briefly—but his children, Carissa and Sammy, would occasionally sail with us, or stay at Marcus' house while I was there. With a growing number of children in the family, it was harder and harder to have a hangover at Marcus' house, so the party mentality of the Caribbean vacations began to subside.

Recognizing that I had already met his entire Caribbean family, Marcus told me casually that he also had an older sister, Michele, who lived in Washington, D.C. I had never met her, even though she lived near us. I later learned that Michele and Hazel knew one another quite well, but I didn't think twice about it.

A few years later, in 2000, Birch & Davis was hosting its annual party at a country club about 30 minutes outside of Washington, D.C. It was an amazing celebratory gala, to which Hazel had invited Michele. Hazel and I were seated at a huge 10-person table when Dad escorted Michele over to us. I had only met Michele once before, at a casual dinner with Dad and Hazel. At that time, I was singing the blues over a failed relationship. At the B&D annual party, I was single and no longer heartbroken.

As Michele made her way to the empty chair in between Hazel and me, Dad said, "You remember my son Damon." Michele said, "Yes; Hi, Damon." Then she sat herself down and promptly turned her back to me, engaging Hazel exclusively. She was telling Hazel the tale of her horrible day to that point. She had a headache, she had locked her keys in the car at her office, and once she finally got into her vehicle, she drove to the party in pouring rain. It sounded like a crappy day to me, and I wondered why she'd bothered showing up to the party at all.

Their conversation broke off when Michele got up to use the ladies' room. I leaned over her vacant chair to get Hazel's attention. Thinking I was keeping my interest secret, I whispered, "Hey, Hazel. What's up with Michele?" Hazel knew I was asking whether she had a boyfriend or not. Hazel leaned over Michele's empty seat too, looked me in the eyes, and asked, "Are you sure you know what you're doing?"

Soon, Michele had returned to the table and Hazel was leaving. Michele and I chatted a little bit, then I asked her to dance. We spent the rest of the party together. As the party drew to a close, Dad stood by the front door shaking hands with his guests as they departed. He was also scanning for guests whom he wanted to continue partying with. He had rented a limousine for the night, so no one had to drink and drive; he could keep the party going, with everyone in one car. When Michele and I reached Dad, he sipped the cocktail in his hand, then asked Michele if she was coming out with us. We looked at one another and she said, "Yeah, sure." At that moment, one of the party guests interrupted us to say farewell. Dad took the opportunity to introduce everyone to each other. "This is my son Damon and his wife Michele." Wife?! Where the hell did that come from? The "girlfriend" thing used to be funny, but *wife*? Whoa. Michele and I looked at one another and uncomfortably laughed it off.

Thankfully, the weather had broken and the deluge outside had stopped. The limo was filling up, and I was getting in to ride with everyone else. Michele had driven herself to the party, so she got in her vehicle to follow the limo downtown. We were almost ready to leave when Hazel blurted out, "Where's Michele?"

"In her car," I said honestly, explaining that she was going to follow.

"Uh-uh; no, no, *no*! You get outta this limo and you go ride with her," Hazel said with a faint slur of intoxication.

The other ladies in the vehicle, smirking, looked on with pursed lips, squinting eyes, and mock disapproval for my presence. Ejected from the limo, I climbed into Michele's passenger seat. We dropped her car off at Dad's house, jumped in the limo with everyone else, and continued to party at bars in downtown D.C. At the end of the night, the limo drove us to the Tastee Diner in Silver Spring for some food to ease the imminent hangovers threatening our mornings. The entire limo full of six other people squeezed themselves into one booth, forcing Michele and I to sit at a table by ourselves. We could hear them giggling, but it was OK. Michele and I definitely liked one another.

The drunken clan stumbled into Dad's house later to watch a movie, but the movie ended up watching us. Everyone passed out except Michele, who stayed awake as people slumped and snored around her, including me. When the movie was over, she woke me up and said she was leaving. Startled and trying to figure out what was going on, I asked why. "Because the movie is over," she replied, dryly stating the obvious.

"But, you can't leave," I said, racking my brain for something to say that would get her to stay.

"Why not?" she shot back in disbelief. I couldn't verbalize a single reason, so I stole a kiss.

Michele and I were married in a small ceremony on the Caribbean island of Nevis, near St. Kitts, in May 2003. I found incredible irony in the fact that I met all my in-laws before I met my wife. I had even met the children we would soon adopt.

At the time, every household in the Ballantyne family had children in the house, but there were two children who were going to need a home. Our niece Carissa and nephew Sammy were hitting adolescence, but their parents were not in their lives. It was clear they were going to need parental support very soon. Carissa and Sammy were the children of Michele's brother Carl. He had passed away at a young age, and their mother had moved away from St. Vincent, leaving her children. Carissa was a beautiful nine-year-old girl, swiftly approaching her teenage years in a male-dominated Caribbean society. Thinking of the children's futures, the family collectively prioritized her needs for structure and love first. Michele and I, while newlywed, had the only home with no children. Since I was adopted, I was very open to Carissa living with us. I was proud of my upbringing with parents who loved and molded me, and we felt like we could offer the same. I felt fortunate for the opportunities I was given and wanted to help other children, especially two I had already met, to have the same opportunities I had.

In December 2003, Marcus brought his family plus Carissa from the Caribbean to the United States for a winter vacation. When they returned to St. Vincent after Christmas, Carissa remained in our care. The morning after Marcus and his family left, Michele and I woke up in our bed and looked at one another. "I guess we have to feed our child," Michele quipped, with happy sarcasm about our new responsibilities. Only seven months after our wedding, we began our journey to becoming adoptive parents. Two years later, when Carissa's younger brother Sammy turned nine years old, Michele and I agreed it would be best to reunite brother and sister. Sammy moved in with us in 2005.

The Adoptee Adopts

Lots of things are challenging for a young, newlywed couple. We had jumped into the deep end, parenting two pre-teens. Michele and I did everything we could to stay positive about our family and our shared decision to provide the children with a better life. But the kids were bitter; they wanted to return to their home country. They wanted their own parents, not substitutes, and didn't like that they had no input in the decisions that were made on their behalf. Those are valid feelings, and many adoptees have them.

Things got challenging in our house. Life was hectic as the children united against us one minute, then battled one another the next. The kids hadn't lived in the same home very often before coming to our house, and they bickered with one another a lot. We knew it was typical behavior between siblings, but it brought an intensity to our house that wasn't present before. The chaos was a significant departure from what I was used to growing up as an only child. What we witnessed was the continuation of their fierce rivalry. One time, when they still lived in the Caribbean, Carissa was prancing along the top of a wall high above their great-grandmother's huge grassy yard below. Sammy, not wanting to be outdone by his sister and always following her wherever she went, also got up on the wall, determined to show her that he could do whatever she could. Rivalry fueled the irritation within Carissa, so she pushed Sammy off the wall. He instinctively put his hands out to try to break his fall, but when his hands hit the ground, his forearms snapped. Carissa ran and hid, leaving him crying on the ground with two broken arms.

As much as they attacked one another, they were also kids who liked to have fun together. Predictably, they shared a sibling comradery that united them against us. That's typical, and we had expected them to band together. But sometimes, their conflicting rivalry and comradery culminated in a perfect storm of confusion. One minute they were ratting one another out to us for the other's transgressions. The next, they were fiercely defending their sibling against our discipline. Some days our interactions with them were dizzying and infuriating.

It was clear they weren't used to the supervision of full-time parents like those Michele and I had grown up with. One day after school, I asked Carissa if she had completed her homework. Of course, her answer was yes.

"May I see it?" I asked, both questioning if she had really completed it and wanting to help correct it if she had.

"Why would you want to see it?" she asked in reply. She wasn't being disrespectful; she was simply confused that someone was holding her accountable for her homework.

Every day, Michele and I remained resolute in the fact that we were doing the right thing for our children. They came to live with us when they were each nine years old, respectively; they'd already had lives and unique experiences that had molded them before we took over as their parents. We hoped that in the future they would appreciate our home and love us as their parents, or at least respect what we tried to do to be a family—but we knew there were no guarantees.

Their adoptions were official in July 2006. Our goal as parents was to help form a stable foundation for their lives, supporting a positive trajectory for their futures. But the road ahead was rough. We also had to navigate the emotional challenges the kids were trying to overcome. When he was very young, Sam had moved from home to home, so stability wasn't anything he was used to when he came to live with us. He had already learned to be independent in other homes, so he tried to rely on himself in ours. Michele asserted that he had also developed a problem with women, so the two of them had issues early on.

One day, I left home to run an errand. Sammy and Michele almost immediately got into an argument. Michele called to report that Sammy had angrily told her that he didn't need us, or any of the things we did for him. He claimed he didn't need anyone. Everything was still new to him and he was trying to cope with his new reality. When I got home, I calmly went upstairs to hear the full story from Michele. We agreed he was feeling lost and probably struggling a lot with living at our house, another in a series of homes in his short life. We wanted to firmly teach him that we were going to do things for him, and it was OK to trust people.

Michele and I recognized that the consequences for his behavior and the message we sent to him in that moment should not suggest that we were sending him away again. He needed to feel he had stability. Children test boundaries and try to assert their independence. That's natural; I get it. I also think it can be harder for an older adoptee to transplant themselves into a new home, being expected to just fit in and accept their new normal. I didn't know that back then, because I was adopted as an infant. I grew up in my family. In Sammy's case, our house likely felt like just another stop before the next place he would live. He probably believed that we wouldn't be together long, so he truly didn't think he needed us.

For middle school, we transitioned Sam from the nurturing private school environment at Lowell School to a public school. Money was tight with two children, and we were thinking about having a third. His public-school classrooms had the classic problem: a 25-to-1 student to teacher ratio made it impossible for the outnumbered, underpaid adult to maintain control and dole out enough discipline to manage the classroom while teaching. Sam immediately picked up on the looser atmosphere in public school. In that first week at his new school, he came home reporting that the other students had been rude to the teacher, but the teacher hadn't disciplined the children. Sam said, "I didn't know we could talk to the teachers like that." When he said that, I knew we were in trouble.

The rest of the year, Sam challenged the teachers' authority, acting out in class and being disrespectful. I received so many calls at work about his behavior that it was hard to focus on my job some days. He was lashing out and being unruly at home, too. His behavior was so disruptive that Michele and I decided he needed way more structure in school and at home than we could provide. We made the very hard decision to transition Sam to Fishburne Military School.

The day we arrived, he was sullen and quiet. The military leadership of the school, dressed immaculately in their respective armed forces uniforms, welcomed him and ushered us through the intake process. Before showing Sam to his room, the intake officer asked if he had any questions. Sam decided to do a litmus test to evaluate just how bad this experience was going to be. He asked the man before him what would happen if he acted in a certain unfavorable way; I don't recall the specific behavior he mentioned. "That's one demerit," the leader responded.

Sam asked his question again, inserting another rule breaking behavior in place of the first. "That's two demerits," the leader replied calmly, but more forcefully. They went back and forth a few times like this, then the leader stopped Sam. He said, "You should know, we post a list of cadets who have earned demerits every day. Right next to that is a list of cadets who have earned merits. Everyone knows who did what, and we're transparent about everyone's behavior." In that moment, I knew Sam was in the right place. There were boundaries in every direction, the school had a firm set of expectations of every cadet's performance, and public lists showed those with infractions alongside those who earned praise.

Of course, he had his ups and downs at school, but his life turned around. He was at home from military school on a break one weekend when we noticed a difference in him. Michele and I began to feel like Sam was going to be all right. As trivial as it sounds, he emptied the dishwasher on his own, without either of us asking him to do so. I never thought I would be so overcome with gratitude for one household chore's completion. Before he left to return to school, Michele helped him pack his bag. She meticulously folded some of his laundry and stuffed snacks in for him to easily stow away when he got back to his room. He said, "Thank you guys so much. You do so much for me. Thanks." It was one of those moments that every parent hopes for: the day your child spontaneously expresses their appreciation for you. It's as if they actually appreciate your presence in their world.

CHAPTER 7

Seth

IN 2007, IN THE MIDST of all the challenges our teenagers presented, Michele and I were also trying to have a child of our own. We hoped that one day her body would show signs of change because it was nurturing a child. When it didn't happen, we realized we needed help. We started the delicate process of fertility treatments. The whole thing was like a complex balancing act, with multiple things to consider at once. Overcoming infertility is an expensive endeavor, and there was no guarantee the treatments would work. But we had to try.

Logistically, Michele and I had to coordinate a series of clandestine consultation appointments during work hours. Of course, we never revealed the truth about where we were going to our colleagues, so there was a lot of "I'm going out, I'll be back in an hour." On Saturdays, we took advantage of the teenagers' natural tendency to sleep in to covertly sneak away for the first available clinic appointments. Mentally, it was stressful to be tested as a couple to learn why we weren't getting pregnant naturally, and what could be done to help us.

We also didn't want to alarm Carissa and Sam with our plans to expand the family. Even though they were our children first, we knew giving birth to our own flesh and blood would raise doubts in their minds about their places in our home. We wanted them to always feel welcome and loved, not fearful that they might be ousted by an infant.

The insertion of our first few embryos was exciting and somewhat stressful. Our fingers and toes were crossed. The procedure went as planned and the doctors monitored her closely. Unfortunately, it didn't work and it took us a while to get over the trauma of our first failed attempt. We were relieved that Michele was healthy, and we were willing to try again.

A few months later, we resumed the regimen of hormone injections. Michele's body had healed from the first round of needle pricks, but soon those injection locations were under attack again. After the second embryo insertion was completed, Michele tried to rest a lot to give her body a safe environment for embryo development. Things were looking good. Her hormone levels were going up, and we felt cautiously optimistic. Sadly, the second attempt failed as well. We were heartbroken to have to go home knowing there would be no child for us after two challenging attempts.

We were emotionally drained, but we knew we had to gather ourselves to press on when the time was right. In the meantime, the older children remained challenging to deal with as we tried to get them on track with everything from proper nutrition and responsibility for their school work to safety in the neighborhood and general respect for us. The entire ordeal was exhausting.

Michele and I were hurt by the near miss we had experienced. Quite naturally we comforted one another emotionally and physically. During that time of healing and loving one another, we made love and bonded even more strongly.

One evening at home, Michele was leaning over my desk as we coordinated family schedules. She stood up with a confused look on her face and complained that she felt funny. We dismissed her feelings at first, but when her discomfort persisted, she said, "I'd better take a pregnancy test." The little white stick showed us a blue "+", bringing us joy we hadn't felt for months. After all we had endured, we had conceived a child naturally.

In the middle of the night on January 15, 2008, Michele managed to lift her pregnant belly from our bed to go to the bathroom and, it seemed to me, turn on every single light she could to get there. I woke up sleepy and confused. I asked with irritation, "Why do you have all the lights on?!" She told me she got up to pee, then she said, "But now I need some help." On her way back to bed, her water had broken. We got her cleaned up, grabbed the "go" bag, and we were on the road to Georgetown University Hospital.

Throughout the night and into the morning, a steady stream of nurses entered the hospital room to check Michele's and the baby's condition. In the morning, the doctors determined the baby's blood pressure was getting low. Michele was instructed to assume all kinds of positions in her bed to relieve the baby's stress. Acting quickly to save our son, the medical staff scheduled a C-section. Without hesitation, Michele accepted the offer of an epidural, which they offered to block the pain from the major procedure she was about to endure. When I saw the size of the needle the nurse was going to insert in Michele's back, I decided the best place for me to look was into Michele's eyes. Soon, she was whisked away to the operating room. I was left in the hospital room alone for so long I thought they'd forgotten about me, and worried I was going to miss the birth.

A nurse finally escorted me to Michele, who was sprawled out on the table with her arms extended straight out, as if she was lying on a cross. A blue paper curtain was tented over her upper chest, blocking her view from the surgery happening on her abdomen. I asked how she was feeling and rubbed the top of her head. She told me she couldn't feel a thing down there, but I could see there was plenty of action. One nurse looked at me very seriously and asked, "You don't get squeamish, do you?"

"No," I said confidently, but secretly I was a little unsure of myself. I had watched a lot of operations on television before, but this was happening in real life—and it was happening to my wife.

"Good," she said, "because we're here for her, not you!" She seemed relieved by my confidence, but it was clear she was trying to scare me into admitting the truth.

"Don't worry about me, I'm good." I tried to reassure her while hoping desperately I really could hold it together.

Michele was awake and talking to me during the procedure. She asked for updates on what was going on beyond the chest screen. I told her, "They just took him out!" She said she had the sensation of pressure being relieved from her stomach and asked how he looked. "He looks like your brother Marcus," I said, referring to the baby's hair. Wet from the womb, it was slicked back in a style similar to my brother-in-law's. "I'll be right back," I told her, then I was gone to see our boy.

Standing in the corner of the operating room, I leaned over the baby warmer to get a better look. I was so entertained by his tiny little cries, protesting the new sensations as air filled his lungs and his body adjusted to being on the outside. I looked over my shoulder back toward Michele, but I was on the other side of the curtain, so I could see everything. I peered past her feet to the area of the incision, then turned back to the nurse next to me at the warmer to ask, "What's that on her stomach?"

"Oh, that's her uterus," the nurse said nonchalantly. "They're about to put it back in." Later I joked with Michele that I know her better than she knows herself, because I've actually seen her uterus and she hasn't!

Back in the hospital room with Michele, everyone was in recovery. Michele from surgery, me from witnessing the life-changing event, and our baby was off with the nurses recovering from the trauma of his surgical extraction. I knew friends and family were waiting for word on how Michele and the baby were doing, so I started making the obligatory phone calls.

Sadly, I was still struggling mightily with Mom's mental health condition and its impact on our relationship. In the moments after our son was born, her state of mind and its consequences hit me in a new way. Our conversations lately on any regular day had consistently been unpredictable, so I was completely unsure what reaction I would get from her when I called to say our son had been born. So, I called Dad first.

Willie was ecstatic when I gave him the news. "Alriiiight, maaan! That's *great*! I'm so happy for you guys!" he declared with excitement. His enthusiasm was awesome, and it was just what I needed to hear. Our chat was brief, but I knew he was already looking forward to being a grandfather. I envisioned him hanging up the phone and sounding the alarm to his friends and family. Dad was exuberant about life in general; when his grandson was born, he didn't disappoint.

I hadn't spoken to Veronica for quite a while, but I knew I had to call with our big news. I braced myself for anything to happen on the phone with her. She could be ecstatic or irrationally unhappy; there was just no way to know. When she answered her phone, she was cordial and congratulatory, but she lacked warm emotions about the delivery of her grandson. In the back of my mind, I recalled how badly she had wanted a grandchild when I was younger. She told me she was going to spoil my kids, and I knew I would have had to let her. She was mentally healthier then, however, and things were much better between us. There on the phone it was clear that she wasn't feeling what was in her heart in the past. Before we hung up, she pledged to come meet her grandson at the hospital soon.

Our son was wheeled into the room in the warmer, swaddled in a blanket. I went over to look at the little addition to our family again, but my gaze was interrupted by a gentle knock at the door. A nurse peered in and said, "Um, someone's father is here…"

I looked at Michele and we smiled, on the verge of laughter. "Oh, that's my Dad!" I told the nurse, just before he sauntered through the door. He was smiling from ear to ear about the new little dude on the Davis team. He waved to Michele and said hello quickly, knowing she wasn't going far, and he could come back to her later. He patted me on the shoulder with a "Hey man!" Then he went straight to his grandson. I joined him and we stood shoulder to shoulder at the side of the baby warmer, marveling at the miracle of life that had come into our world.

On day two, our nurse wheeled our boy into the room to be with us again. He spent the night in their care, allowing Michele to rest. The identification label on his little bed read *Baby Boy Ballantyne*. We had a name picked out for him, but when I looked at him closely, the name just didn't fit. He remained nameless for three days while we thought hard about a more suitable one. On the third day, we decided he looked like a "Seth". Seth Nathaniel Davis.

A C-section is a major procedure that can be challenging to recover from; Michele stayed at the hospital for three days to do so. During that time, she struggled to do many things she'd previously done effortlessly, before Seth was born. Sitting up in bed or walking to the bathroom unassisted were major accomplishments. Midway through her hospital recovery, she exclaimed sarcastically, "You don't realize how much you use your abs until someone slices them open!"

By the time we were discharged to go home on day three, Veronica had still not made it to the hospital to meet Seth. A week or so after we settled in at home, I called her again to see if she could finally bring herself to meet her grandson. I wanted to keep trying to connect with her. I felt it was crucial to take advantage of this huge life event, hopefully appealing to her deepest emotions to make a connection. Seth was growing daily, and the moments she was missing were precious. Dad stopped by every day, loving his grandson more and more, imprinting his influences in Seth's head. He tugged at Seth's little legs and tucked his pinky finger into Seth's tightly clenched fists. I really wanted Mom to experience the joy we were feeling, too. When she finally agreed on a date to come meet the little guy, she didn't come. I knew she wouldn't, but it still hurt.

Months passed before I tried again. Finally, to my astonishment, Veronica actually showed up. I had mixed emotions about her visit, and I was nervous something would erupt between us. I was glad she came, but I was tense during her visit. I kept wondering what she might hallucinate in our home that I would be forced to deal with in front of Seth. When she came in, she put her purse on the steps and immediately reached for her grandson. Veronica snuggled him in her arms, cooed baby talk at him, and made goofy noises. I took a few pictures of them together during those moments that I cherish to this day.

A few days later, Mom called to tell me that she thought our nanny had gone into her purse while she was in the bathroom. I didn't argue with her, even though I knew for a fact the incident had not happened. Veronica and Seth haven't seen one another since, and apparently, she moved to Raymore, MO a few months later. I talk to Seth about Nanna Veronica to keep her memory alive in his mind, but he has no idea who she is. Mental illness robbed Mom of one of the many joys mothers look forward to when raising their own children: becoming a grandmother.

Thankfully, Dad lived very close to us in Silver Spring, MD and our proximity was great for his connection to Seth. There were days when I got home from work to find Dad's bright red Mercedes convertible already parked in the driveway. It always made me smile to know that he was so invested in seeing his grandson and being a part of his life.

CHAPTER 8

Happy to Be at Home

WHEN SETH WAS BORN, I was working as a contractor at the Centers for Medicare and Medicaid Services. The commutes between Baltimore and Silver Spring were long, but I was driving opposite rush hour traffic, so it could have been much worse. Regardless, the time I spent on the road was time I was missing at home with the family. Rumors of a layoff were swirling throughout the office, so everyone was nervous about losing their job. I was not the primary breadwinner in our home, but I was a contributor; with two teenagers and a baby to care for, I was concerned about how well we would navigate the fiscal challenges of being a single income home. Michele reassured me that if I lost my job, our family would be all right. When the call came, my bosses were apologetic because they knew we'd just had a baby. I was disappointed to be released, but I was relieved the suspense was over. I didn't love the job and only felt connected to a few of my colleagues, so I didn't feel a big loss. The next chapter of my life was unwritten, but one thing was clear: I would have a lot more time at home with Seth.

Most parents don't have the gift of extended time at home with their newborn baby. Truthfully, I felt very fortunate to be able to spend time with him while he was still an infant. So often, we're pressured by fears of job or financial insecurity and we're forced back to work too quickly.

I was there to care for him every day, playing with him and nurturing him. On one of those days when we boys were at home alone, I was sitting in our living room chair, hovering over Seth as he lay on his back on the ottoman in front of me. He was dressed in a onesie that covered his feet, kicking uncontrollably in the air. His hands swatted in every direction as he tested his motor skills. He stared up at me as I stared down and spoke to him. I didn't speak baby talk; I used my regular voice in a monologue to my son. I wondered aloud what he would be when he grew up, talking about all the hopes and dreams I had for him. I told him I hoped I would be the best father possible to help get him there, wherever that turned out to be. That's when it hit me.

My eyes welled up with tears and I was overcome with emotion. I fell silent for a few moments and just stared, almost in disbelief, at my son. My voice cracked when I broke the silence.

"You're the first blood relative I've ever known," I mumbled.

I cried warm tears of joy and astonishment. I had never truly contemplated the fact that I had gone my entire life without knowing a single person with whom I shared a blood relation. I finally realized what adoption actually meant, and the thought floored me. *My parents are my family, but there are people out there who are part of an entirely different family that I don't know, and that I'm a part of.* Squirming before me, Seth represented a living incarnation of my life's reality. That moment solidified an idea I had kept in the back of my mind for a while: I wanted to find my other family.

After several months at home with Seth, I returned to the work force. In the summer of 2008, I took another contracting job at the Internal Revenue Service. I had worked there before, and we busted our asses in that job. When I left the first time, I felt that I had done my time and was sure the IRS days were behind me. Returning to work there, I had mixed emotions; I was glad to be employed, but I wished it was somewhere else. Unfortunately, my gut reaction to accepting the job was correct: I hated it. After six months of job dissatisfaction, Michele and I agreed I should resign, because new job opportunities were on the horizon.

The year 2008 turned out to be huge. Our son was born, I was laid off from a job, and I had committed to searching for my birth family. In the middle of it all, on August 28, Barrack Obama accepted the Democratic nomination to run for president of the United States. On the night of November 4, Michele and I sat on the end of our bed staring at the television, with Seth sleeping behind us. At the end of a challenging presidential race versus Republican nominee John McCain, we hoped that the next president wouldn't just represent us, but would actually look like us as well. My eyes welled up as President-elect Obama delivered his acceptance speech in Grant Park in Chicago. I turned around to have a look at our son, an infant sleeping in the middle of a king-sized bed. I crawled onto the bed, kissed him gently on the head, and said, "We did it, buddy; we got you a black president." It was a moment of pride for many people across the nation and around the world. I couldn't have known then I would be granted a chance to be a small part of that historical presidential administration. In June of 2009, I went to work at the U.S. Department of Health and Human Services in the Office of the National Coordinator for Health IT. I felt very fortunate that Michele's connections afforded me that opportunity. While I was proud to be a part of the administration, I didn't know yet how important the location of that job—in downtown Washington, D.C.—would be.

CHAPTER 9

THE SEARCH

THE IDEA TO LAUNCH a search for my relatives was planted in my head in the years preceding Seth's birth. Back in the summer of 2007, my father-in-law Freddy traveled to the east coast of the United States from St. Vincent. (He always has several segments to his travel plans and that time he made it to Silver Spring to visit us. He also wanted to see his distant cousin Leona in Baltimore, so we made the 45-minute drive north to her home in the city. Leona lived in an older neighborhood, where it was clear her home had been there for decades. The sidewalk leading to her front door was uneven from years of growing tree roots and shifting soil underneath. The greenish-blue color of her house was faded by pounding weather and years of intense sun.

She greeted us warmly at the front door and invited us inside. As she turned slowly, extending her hand toward the living room for us to go sit down, I noticed she was towing an oxygen tank on wheels behind her, with tubes laced over her ears and under her nose. The apparatus was a signal of her elderly state; Leona was in the autumn of her life.

We made small talk about how nice it was to meet her, and shared a little bit about how everyone had been. She asked about people who lived back in St. Vincent. Then the conversation shifted to story-telling about their family members. As she spoke, her deep historical knowledge of the family's experiences filled the room with vivid imagery while we sat quietly and listened. As she recounted the past, she pulled a box from under her coffee table that contained a collection of artifacts supporting every story. Huddled around the table, she showed us handwritten letters, old photographs, and well-preserved newspaper clippings. She pointed to each item one by one, and we passed them to each other as she spoke. The table was covered in graduation announcements and funeral programs that she linked to people and places she and Freddy knew well. If someone was born, got married, or died, she knew where everyone else in the family was around that same time. As the table filled with the family's historical artifacts, I was struck by how this elderly woman pieced together their family's history in a way I was sure few others could.

Watching her weave the story of their family's journey helped me see a stark reality with dire implications for my own life. If I didn't investigate my biological family's history and try to find my people, someone just like cousin Leona among them would transition from this life and take their knowledge and our stories with them. I needed to seize the opportunity to make some connections before those opportunities vanished forever.

The urge to learn who my birth mother was bubbled up within me more fiercely than it ever had before. Coincidentally, my friend Kelly had recently asked me if I wanted to find my biological mother. She had suggested embarking on the journey more than once over the years, so I was mildly irritated that she was raising the subject again. Kelly later admitted that witnessing the deterioration of my relationship with Veronica made her think I could benefit from learning more about my birth family. As much as I hated to admit it, she was right—and sitting with cousin Leona was an unmistakable sign. For the rest of our visit with her, my mind was focused on how I could launch a search for my birth mother.

But in the days after that wonderful visit, my enthusiasm to start a search deflated somewhat. I was having second thoughts, so I paused and took a step back to reflect on how I was doing mentally. I asked myself several times if I was truly ready for the search. Mom and I had been through a lot in recent years, and I was very unhappy with the situation. In my excitement to find my people, I hadn't stopped to think about how her mental state was affecting me. I also hadn't contemplated how she would take the news that I was launching a search. She was already hallucinating about people who didn't exist trying to harm her; how would she react if I told her I was looking for my birth mother? Would she still be as supportive as she had pledged to be when I was a child? Or would the voices in her head turn her against me and my quest? I tried to determine if I was launching my search for the right reasons, examining my feelings deeply. I had to be completely confident that I wanted to find this woman because I truly wanted to find her, and not because I wanted to replace my mother, who had been stolen from me by mental illness.

Introspection consumed my thoughts for days. As I passed by the mirror in my bathroom one evening, I leaned on the counter and looked myself in the eye. I asked myself, out loud, "Are you sure you're doing this for the right reasons?" The answer was yes; I still felt strongly that I wanted to learn more about my blood relatives. I challenged my resolve from a different angle, asking, "What will happen if Mom flips out on me?" I told myself I would have to go it alone as best I could, in that case. I thought about the adoption documentation she had retained, and I wondered if it could assist my search. But if she wasn't willing to supply those artifacts, I would have to press on without them. I still needed answers, so finally, after several days of reflection, I decided I was definitely going forward with my search for the right reasons, and I was all in.

I gathered my composure and called Mom a few days later. After the obligatory small talk, I let her know what I was thinking. "Remember how you've always told me that if I ever wanted to search for my birth mother, you would be happy to help?" I prodded, trying to help her recall saying that. "Well, I think I'm ready to search for her," I said, holding my breath as I waited for her reaction.

"OK," she said, matter-of-factly. "Then I'll need to get the papers I have together and send them to you." She launched into a stream of chatter, listing every artifact that she had: entries in my baby book, legal adoption papers, and more. She was speaking with frenetic excitement in her voice; I didn't know if I should be concerned for how nervous her reaction was, or excited by how energized and willing to assist me in the search she seemed to be. When we hung up the phone, I had mixed emotions. It was a relief that she said she would help. I was in disbelief that she took the news of my search so well, and I was nervous that she wouldn't follow through on her word—then turn against me, to boot. Thankfully, Mom found it within herself to gather every piece of information she could find about my adoption, make copies, and drop them promptly in the mail to me. They weren't much, but it was enough to get me started and I was so thankful to have them. Most importantly, receiving the documents in the mail was an affirmation of Mom's unwavering support for me to find my biological family one day. It meant more to me than she will ever know.

In November 2008, I called the Baltimore's city' social services office to learn more about the process of launching a search. I had no idea what was required, nor what I was getting myself into. They mailed me an adoptee pre-search informational package, and a questionnaire filled with probing inquiries that tried to get a feel for why I was searching. The questions that explored how I was feeling about starting my search weren't challenging at all, because I had already contemplated my feelings so thoroughly. A few of the questions are listed below:

Question 2: What are your expectations/goals for this search?

Answer: *I just want to meet them, or at least see pictures of relatives to see who I look like. I'm interested to know why I was put up for adoption, and I want them to be able to rest their minds that I am OK.*

Question 6: If you don't like your birthmother, birthfather, sister or brother, how will you feel? What will you do?

Answer: *I already have family, friends, and a full life with my own kids. If I don't like who I find, I will let the relationship fade and not worry about it."* (That answer turned out to be oddly prophetic.)

Question 21: Do you want a relationship with your birthmother or birthfather?

Answer: *Maybe; I have a mother and father, so we'll see how things go.*

I returned my completed questionnaire in December 2008. Within a few days, I got a call from my assigned social worker, Lee Burress. She had a soft voice that instantly put me at ease. I sensed wisdom in her caring demeanor, and it was clear that she'd had a lot of experience in assisting reunions. She asked questions about me, my life, and the reasons for my search at that moment in time. I can only assume she must have been trying to verify the answers I provided on the questionnaire, evaluating my sincerity as I repeated them during our call. I reiterated for her that I had a very well-adjusted upbringing, with two loving parents. I reassured her that I had no ailments, maladies, or diseases, and that there was no sad story prompting my investigation into the vaults of my personal history. I joyfully shared that Michele and I had just had a son, and being face to face with the first blood relative I had ever known made me hungry for more information. Lee explained that in her experience, there are several factors that influence a person's desire to search for their biological relatives: generally female children begin their search earlier in life than males, but males are often prompted by the birth of their own children, as I had been.

Lee forewarned me the process could take a very long time. Of course, I had to sign additional paperwork to even get started. She invited me to her office in Baltimore to meet, sign some consent forms, and take home the informational packet to review how the process worked. She reminded me it was going to be a bit of an investigation that could take quite a while. The first phase was to simply find the file containing my original adoption records. I envisioned a huge warehouse, just like the final scene of the movie *Indiana Jones and the Raiders of the Lost Ark*, stacked to the soaring ceiling full of boxes and records that hadn't been touched for decades. There must have been millions of artifacts of people's lives stowed away somewhere in archives of documents, waiting to be to be of service to someone.

It took months for Lee to obtain the paper records. She reviewed the notes of my case and drafted a synopsis of the circumstances that brought me into the agency's care. Lee was required to de-identify everyone involved to maintain their anonymity, at least until she'd had a chance to contact them. If the time ever came, Lee would also serve as an intermediary between me and whomever she found. Until then, all I could do was accept her invitation back to her office to read her report.

I never dwelled on it, but I was curious about why I was put up for adoption. I was born in Baltimore in the 1970s. Growing up hearing about the crack epidemic of the 1980s and '90s, I had wondered if I was a drug baby from an earlier epidemic. Somehow that didn't seem right, if my birthmother was a librarian and my birthfather was a cop. Had my mother been raped? My buddy Andre told me that he was the product of such a violent crime; could the same be true for me? I had no answers, so whenever I was curious about my origins, I was left to just make stuff up in my mind. However, I always realized quickly it was a useless exercise, so I repeatedly talked myself out of imagining any more scenarios. On this special occasion that I had initiated, I was looking forward to finally hearing the facts about my early life from Lee, and escaping the scenarios I'd conjured up in my imagination.

I arrived at Lee's building in east Baltimore and calmly cleared building security, then sat alone among rows and rows of blue chairs in the waiting room. I imagined all the families who had passed through that waiting room before me, with various challenging problems and pressing needs. There I was, simply wanting more information about myself.

When Lee opened the lobby door I stood up to greet her, smiling as I shook her hand and thanked her for her work. Her eyes twinkled with a joy for moments like these in her career, and a humble pride for helping people along their life's journey. I knew she had likely assisted hundreds of cases before mine, and that there would be many more to come. But in that moment, I felt like she was completely focused on me and what I needed. Lee escorted me to a small conference room with a modest table and chairs, a few old pictures on the walls depicting calming scenic outdoor views, and a bin of toys in the corner. It was easy to imagine the families who sat in this room and hoped their children would be entertained by those toys as the parents handled much more serious matters at the table.

Lee left me alone in the room briefly, returning with my file in her hand. She had two copies of the report she had compiled about my adoption. She slid one copy across the table to me, retaining the other so she could read along and answer questions.

The document was titled *Background Information from the Agency's Closed Birth Parent Record for Michael, Born 1972*. It was divided into four sections: *Birth History, Reason You Came to the Attention of this*

Agency, *Birth Family History*, and *Foster Care History*. I was already fascinated. I was only expecting information about why I was placed in the care of the agency and then into adoption, so the three additional history sections were an exciting surprise. I read the report silently, trying to comprehend as many details as I could all at once.

"You were born via Caesarean section after a long and difficult labor," the Birth History section revealed. Later, when I thought back on that fact, I related Michele's C-section with Seth to Ann's C-section when I was born: like father like son. I reminisced on Michele's challenging recovery, and her exasperated exclamation about the importance of her stomach muscles in her daily life. In that moment, I learned what my mother had endured more than 30 years prior. And, like Michele, that she had lived with a scar that represented my life for the rest of her days.

Reading further, I learned that my biological mother met with the social services office on September 25, 1972 and was *emphatic that she wished to pursue adoption*. I learned she was 26 at the time and had just completed graduate school in the field of library sciences. Graduate school meant she was intelligent; that was good news to me. The report said, "She disclosed that while she was in school in another state, she became involved with a man residing in the city where she was attending school. Your birth mother ended her relationship with this man after an incident where he took advantage of her. She later discovered that your birth father was married when she called his place of employment, and she was asked if she was his wife calling."

Part of my truth was finally revealed. My mother had unknowingly found herself mixed up in an extra-marital affair and had gotten pregnant but wasn't supported by the biological father. Those facts brought my adoption into focus and clarified my mission in seeking reunion; I would only be searching for my biological mother. The man who helped conceive me was not involved in any of the plans for my well-being from the moment he learned I was coming, so there was no reason to locate him.

My birth family history surprised me a bit. "Your birth mother was born in Kentucky, but her family moved to the Eastern Shore of Maryland shortly thereafter." Kentucky? Fascinating. I couldn't recall a single time in my life when I thought twice about the state of Kentucky, but at that moment, I learned my roots were there and on the Eastern Shore of Maryland.

"She had brown eyes, auburn hair, and a light complexion," the report stated. I had a hard time visualizing her in that moment, because the other details were so captivating. I kept reading.

"She was described by the agency social worker as warm and outgoing, while handling her unplanned pregnancy with an analytical approach rather than an emotional one." That description really resonated with me, because it sounded like a description of myself. I've never been one for emotional decisions. A calm, collected, logical approach is how I attack any situation, and it sounded like I got those traits from my mother. I was beginning to feel just a little bit closer to her than I had before.

Finally, I read the Foster Care History. It was one of the smaller sections in the report, but it turned out to be one of the most poignant, because it described me during the transition between my biological mother and my adopted parents. The report quoted from my adoption court file, stating, "Michael maintained good health… He is a happy, alert baby, very even tempered and lovable… He has even features, and overall gives the appearance of a handsome baby." It was comforting to read those kind words, even 36 years later. Knowing I was in good health, in good spirits, and already exhibiting some of the personality traits that make me who I am today was somehow validating. I've always been me, no matter what my name was, no matter whose care I was in.

But the most moving part for me was a parallel I saw between myself and my son. Reading the description of myself in foster care was like reading a description of Seth as a baby. I was in tears.

Who Am I Really?

I reached for the tissue box on the table, and Lee asked if I was OK. I smiled through overflowing eyes and told her yes. She gave me some time to process my emotions after learning about myself from her report. There was clearly so much more to the story, but from that point I had way more information than I had ever known before. Once I calmed myself down from the raw emotion of learning where I came from, Lee gently sent me on my way with homework to do. My next task was to write an introductory letter to my biological mother introducing myself.

When I thought about it later, I realized reading about my first days as an infant from the report prepared by Lee, a third party who wasn't present at the time, was very unnatural. In a "traditional" family, a child's parents can tell them all sorts of specific stories about the months, weeks, and days leading up to their birth, and the time they shared together thereafter. Seth used to ask Michele about his own birth often. He wanted to hear how it was for her to carry him inside her womb. He wanted to know about her C-section, and what his first little cries sounded like to our ears. Adopted kids don't usually have any of that poignant information about themselves. We're left to imagine and fantasize, creating stories of who our parents might be, how our lives might have begun, and if we were (or are) loved by our birth parents.

I went to work that day and sequestered myself in my cubicle. The walls only went ¾ of the way to the ceiling, and everyone could hear everyone else's conversations effortlessly throughout the office. But my cubicle was completely silent, except for the occasional clicking of my computer keyboard. I was inside my head, drafting exactly what I wanted to say. My mind was laser focused on the messages I wanted to convey and choosing exactly the right words to say to the woman who gave me life. In any other situation, I have the utmost confidence when introducing myself to a stranger. But I knew the introduction I was drafting would make an indelible impression, so it had to be perfect. I wanted the lasting impact to be reassurance that she had made the right decision, in allowing me to live. I felt she'd want to know that I had been deeply loved since the last time she saw me. My goal was to convey that I was open to knowing her, if that was her desire too, and that in her own time, I would welcome the opportunity to meet her. I spent the entire afternoon crafting what I hoped would be a comforting introduction that reassured her I had turned out just fine. I read that letter over and over on my screen to make sure everything I typed was exactly the word I wanted to use. It was the most important thing I had ever written, and I only had one chance to make my first impression. When it was finished, I printed it, then sat back down to transcribe it in my own handwriting.

The letter read:

> *You must be filled with so much anticipation and emotion for what I have to say to you after 36 years. I'll start with my deepest, most heartfelt thank you. I have boundless and infinite gratitude for the life I've led, because you decided that you wanted a better life for me. If you've ever felt unsure about your decision so long ago, please take comfort in knowing that I quickly landed in loving, nurturing arms and that everything worked out just fine. I hope it brings you joy to know that the baby boy you once knew, Michael, is all grown up as a healthy young man.*
>
> *If you're wondering, "Why is he looking for me now?" the answer is very simple. During a visit with my in-laws, one of the older members of the family told stories and was able to detail family history that was invaluable to their family tree. Some simple curiosities were sparked by the elder in-law's amazing ability to recount family members' lives. It was then that I realized that I wanted to try to find out more of my personal information.*

Who Am I Really?

Along those lines, I fully recognize that it may be somewhat painful and unexpectedly emotional to begin to think about this situation all over again. It was emotional for me to read the circumstances for my adoption plan; however, I'm very relieved to finally have those answers. I fully acknowledge that we both have well-established lives, and I don't wish to disrupt yours. Above all else, I just wanted you to know that I am just fine. I'd love the opportunity to talk someday, but please take your time in figuring out when you're ready for that. We've waited this long...

To let you know where I've been in my life, I grew up not too far from Baltimore. After graduating from high school, I attended Hampton University, where I earned a B.S. in business. Soon after graduation, I attended Loyola College where I earned a Master's in Business Administration. I worked in the IT field for many years; however, I recently seized an opportunity to work on an assignment for the Obama Administration.

I got married in 2003. We've since adopted two children from my wife's side of the family, and we have one beautiful little boy of our own, born in 2008. He is the absolute pride and joy of my world.

My personality is warm and outgoing. I like people, and I get along with nearly everyone I meet. I'm lucky that way. My disposition is calm, laid back, and casual. My general disposition is that life is good, and there just aren't that many things that truly stress me out. My "glass" is a little more than half full in most instances. I'm thankful to have a positive outlook on nearly everything. I love to laugh, and even in the most adverse situation, I can usually find a joke, even if it's at my own expense.

So, take your time. I know this is a lot to contemplate. My only hope is that someone is able to find you and they're able to convey to you that your boy is thriving, and you absolutely made the right decision. I'll be just fine with that. However, I will welcome any contact you feel up to, when the time is right for you.

Once that was finished, I left the office feeling drained and relieved. It had been a long, emotional day. I had said exactly what I wanted to say, and there was nothing more I could do. When I got home, I enclosed both copies of the letter in an envelope, added a picture of Michele and me on our wedding day, and a recent photo of Seth, who was a toddler at the time. The next morning, I walked one block from our house down Spring Street, to a mailbox on the corner of Fairview Road. It was practically right in front of Dad's former Birch & Davis building. I dropped the letter in the box and walked away. "Well, that's that," I said out loud to myself, smacking my hands up and down a few times, officially signaling that my job was done. Inside my head, I reminded myself that I hadn't given reunification much thought for 36 years, so I wasn't about to let the fantasies or anxieties take over my life at that point. There was no guarantee my biological mother could ever be found, or that my letter would reach anyone who even cared.

Ann:

"Friday, September 11, 2009, I stayed after work and hung out with some friends, something that was definitely not a part of my routine. I didn't feel like stopping to pick up the mail. The box was probably filled with junk as usual, so I decided it could wait.

I fooled around all day Saturday and didn't think about the mail again until later that evening. I was right; there was nothing but junk—and a brown envelope.

"I sifted through the junk first and moved on to the dreaded brown envelope. I expected some unwanted information, or a problem that I would have to resolve. *No good news comes in a brown business envelope*, I thought.

"The return address was the Office of Social Services in Baltimore. I was sure it was some sort of mistake until I opened the envelope and began to read. I saw the year 1972, and suddenly I knew it was the moment I had been waiting for 36 years. I started to shake from head to toe. My eyes filled with tears, and it was hard to read the words. I could only hope that it was good news.

"I read the letter several times before I realized that I would have to wait until Monday morning to call the office and get confirmation that my son was looking for me. I remember reading the letter over and over, trying to be absolutely sure that I had read it right. I don't remember sleeping. I am sure I passed out from emotional exhaustion alone, at some point.

"The next morning, I tried to be normal and just get through the day. I went to the barber shop to get a haircut. I sat down in Lisa's chair. There were three young men sitting near her and talking with her. She introduced them as her sons. They talked about a cousin who had been injured on the first play of a football game on Saturday. I quietly started to cry as I thought about my son, and how little I knew about him. I remained silent and fled the premises as soon as I was done.

"I spent the rest of Sunday planning what I would do Monday morning. I was not scheduled to work that day, so I decided to get up early, shower, and get dressed in case I had to drive to

Baltimore the next day. Another night passed, and I don't know how I managed to sleep. The next morning, I couldn't eat. I sat at the dining room table with the phone, waiting for 8:30 a.m. when the office would be open, and I could make the call.

"Lee Burris was at her desk when I called at 8:35 a.m. She was warm and calm as she asked me if I knew what the letter was about. I rattled off the details, and I could hear her smile when she confirmed that my son was looking for me. When I hung up, I knew to expect some legal papers in the mail, with forms to fill out and instructions to follow that would get the process started.

"And so, the waiting began. The package of materials arrived on Saturday. The anticipation nearly smothered me. I knew it contained legal documents to be completed and notarized, but it also contained the standard letter from the adoptee to the birth parent and some pictures. I went to the bedroom with the mail, then opened everything but the one item I had been waiting for. When everything else had been dealt with, I gently opened the letter and pulled the contents out a little bit. I saw about half an inch of a photo, put the envelope on the bed, and walked out of the room as if I wasn't excited. I think I did that several times. Finally, it was time to find out what I had to face.

"The pictures fell out of the envelope and into my lap. The first thing I saw was a beautiful baby, holding onto and standing between his daddy's legs. My first words were "I'm a grandmother!" It took a moment to move on to the picture of my son and his bride.

"There he was: handsome beyond belief, with a beautiful bride and a son. This was more than I was expecting. I don't know how long I stared at the pictures, but eventually, my focus went to getting the paperwork done and in the mail to Lee. Now that I had seen my son for the first time, I was ready to read his letter.

"Still trembling, I started to read: 'So much anticipation and emotion…' 'Deepest, most heart-felt thank you…' 'Wanted a better life for me…' My heart was not prepared to receive these words. I had spent so many years second-guessing my decision, wondering why I could not see a way to keep my child as other mothers had, regardless of their circumstances. I continued to read, looking for some sign of negative emotions. 'I just wanted you to know that I am fine. Your boy is thriving, and you absolutely made the right decision.'

"I carefully laid the letter aside to avoid staining it with my tears. I cried so hard that I could hardly breathe. I paced, unable to sit still. My fate was sealed. After nearly thirty-seven years, the moment I had dreamed of and longed for was at hand. I tried to imagine what I wanted to happen, but it was too soon to go there. I had yet to hear his voice. I had yet to write my own letter. As the years passed, I had locked away my emotions so tightly that I was not sure how I would find the words I needed to say.

"The weekend was ahead of me and I was sure I had plenty of time to fill out the forms, write the letter, and put the package in the mail on my way to work on Monday morning. By 2 a.m. Monday, it was apparent that I had underestimated how hard writing this letter would be. After a few hours of sleep, I called in sick and worked through the day. Early Tuesday morning, the package was on its way to Lee.

"For the next twenty-four hours, I flipped back and forth thinking of the potentially positive and negative outcome that could evolve after my son received my letter and photos. I told myself that there would be time to prepare for our meeting. I remembered stories I had seen on TV, of reunions between birth parents and children, and tried to imagine where and when the big event would occur. From the moment my package dropped into the mailbox, I walked around in a daydream. I told no one about what was going on in my life."

CHAPTER 10

"36 Years…"

TWO WEEKS AFTER I dropped my introductory letter in the mail, Lee's phone number appeared as an incoming call on my mobile phone. I stared at it for a few seconds, thinking, *she couldn't have news already*. But she did. In her quiet, nurturing voice, Lee said, "I just got off the phone with your biological mother, and she's ecstatic to know that you want to be in contact with her." The shock I felt for the rapid turn of events was mixed with a wave of relief that my instinct to reach out to her had been correct. There was genuine comfort in knowing she was receptive to hearing from me and was excited that I was looking for her.

Fear of rejection is a major challenge for adoptees who want to launch a search for their biological relatives. For some, the fear that their birth family won't want to be in contact with them is so great that they never search at all. In that moment, the hurdle of fear was behind me. I revealed to Lee that I'd found it cathartic to go through the process of drafting my introductory letter to my biological mother. Reflecting on the writing experience, I told her it allowed me a chance to think very carefully about my emotions, how I wanted to present myself to her, and how to thank her for the opportunities that my life afforded me. I asked Lee if she would request a similar letter from my birthmother.

Who Am I Really?

On September 23, 2009, only one week later, Lee called again. I was walking in the halls of the Hubert H. Humphrey federal building; I happened to be in between meetings and resolving a long to-do list of work stuff, but I stopped everything to hear what Lee had to say. She had my mother's letter in her possession, and she wanted to know if I wanted her to mail it to me, or if she should read it over the phone. I wanted to hear it immediately, but I knew I had to exit the office quickly to find somewhere that I could be alone. I get emotional about stuff and my heart strings are easily pulled, so I knew that hearing this letter was guaranteed to turn on a set of waterworks like nothing I had experienced before. I asked Lee to give me a few minutes to find a place of solitude, and I would call her right back. I rushed out of the building and went straight to the outdoor botanical gardens off Independence Ave. I found a lone bench tucked into a shady nook, mostly out of the view of passersby. Cars were whizzing past on the street behind me, but when I returned Lee's call, all I could hear was her voice. She had been so sweet and comforting during the entire process, and in that moment, her soft voice acted as a surrogate for my birth mother's.

"Damon,

"My name is Ann, and I'm your birthmother. Thank you for the beautiful letter you wrote to me. Your words were filled with sincerity, respect, comfort, and concern for my feelings. It tells me a lot about the person that you are.

"Thank you so much for the beautiful pictures I received. You are remarkably handsome and your bride, Michele, is so elegant, and simply lovely. As if seeing you wasn't enough, seeing Seth took my breath away. What a beautiful family you have!

"I am very excited—to say the least—that you wish to be in touch with me. I wanted our contact to be your decision, made when you were ready. Before you were born I promised that, out of respect for your best interest, I would leave this decision to you. In 2002, I did lots of research on how to locate a birth child, but chose not to take action because that would mean breaking what I knew was a sacred promise.

"Let me assure you that there are no negative feelings or circumstances waiting to be revealed. I have no regrets, even though for your first year of life I struggled with the urge to take you back. The only thing that stopped me was knowing that the bond between you and your parents had already formed. My selfish action would have broken that bond, and I did not want to do you or your newly formed family any harm.

"I come from a loving family and a well-balanced life. My father was a teacher and my mother a beautician. I have an older sister, Adeline, who is divorced. She has one daughter, Mary Ann, who is married to Franklin, and two grandchildren: Kyle and Kayla. We have oodles of cousins in Kentucky. In the summer of 2001, Adeline and I found out that we had an older brother: my father's son, whose name is Bill. He lives in Chicago with his second wife Chris, and has four children, five grandchildren, and two great-grandchildren.

"I was born September 24, 1946 in Kentucky but grew up in Maryland. I also attended Hampton, but I was an immature and naïve little country girl who forgot about studying because smoking cigarettes and playing double-deck pinochle was much more fun! Consequently, I flunked out of Hampton, even though I was third in my high school graduating class. This was a pivotal point in my life, because Daddy told me I would have to find the money to finish college—and I did. I graduated from Kentucky State University in 1971 with a BA in English and a minor in French.

"I graduated Wayne State University in August of 1972 with a master's degree in library science, and you on the way. My best friend, who lived in Baltimore and was a social worker, helped me get on welfare—which meant that I had a lovely little studio apartment, health care, and Baltimore's assistance with arranging for your adoption.

"You were born by Caesarean section around 1 p.m. on Saturday, October 14, 1972, if I remember correctly. I saw you kicking on the table where the nurses were cleaning you before you went to the nursery. You were named Michael Anthony, and the nurse told me you were born with blond hair and blue eyes. (My Daddy told me that I was born with blond hair and blue eyes too, but my hair turned red within a week. His pet name for me was Carrot Top.) My nurse told me that you passed all your "new baby" tests with scores of 9 or 10, out of 10!

"As soon as all procedures for your adoption were completed, I turned in my welfare credentials and made my way home to my mother and father (who was seriously ill at the time). I married in 1975 and divorced in 1985, but I do not have any other children.

"Today, I am a librarian working for the federal government. As a result of my marriage to a member of the Air Force, I have lived in Delaware, Kentucky, California, and Maryland. I have also lived in Zaragoza, Spain for two years and in Wiesbaden, Germany for seven years. In addition, I have visited Canada, France, Belgium, Holland, Italy, Switzerland, Austria, Andorra, and the Republic of San Marina. I have also visited the

Ivory Coast and Nigeria. I share with you the ability to get along with almost everyone. I believe in helping people, and love to perform "random acts of senseless kindness." As you might guess, I love to read and in addition, I am an amateur calligrapher, photographer, poet, and family genealogist.

"I am grateful to your father and mother for giving you a home filled with love and a wonderful life. That is what I hoped for, when I released you with all of the love I had in my heart. I have had an ongoing conversation with you all of your life. I have sent you love and the message that you would be welcomed with open arms, should you decide to make contact. When I became friends with anyone, I would eventually tell them about placing you in adoption. I would tell my friend that if anyone ever came looking for me and asked if I had a child, please tell them yes and where to find me, because I wanted to be found.

"And now, finally, I am found.

"Your birthmother,

Ann"

I sat on the bench sobbing gently, with tears streaming down my face. Lee had found my birth mother, her name was Ann, and she'd just told me so much of what I wanted to hear.

At the end of the reading, Lee asked if I was OK. I assured her that I was fine; then, I asked her what happened next. She told me she would mail Ann's letter to me, and asked if I was ready to write down Ann's phone number, adding that with my permission, she would also give Ann my phone number. After I wrote Ann's number down, Lee said it was up to Ann and me to figure out how we wanted to proceed. She was signaling that she was stepping aside, that it was up to us to figure out the next steps that were right for both of us.

I thanked Lee profusely for reading the letter telling her she was exactly the person I needed to read my mother's words to me. When we hung up, I cried openly with my hands covering my face. Ann had specifically said she was glad I was looking for her. I wanted to call her immediately, but I knew I couldn't call right then. It was early afternoon; if she picked up the phone, we'd both cry uncontrollably, and we could never return to our jobs to finish out the work day. Still, I wanted her to know in that very moment that we were connected. There was no way to call and only leave a message; she might actually answer the phone, and I had no idea what I would even say. I decided to send her a text message, but I still had no clue what the right words were. I needed something that could truly only come from me at that moment. I tapped out: "*36 years...*" She would surely know that was from me.

Ann:

"Wednesday morning, I had calmed down a bit. I moved through the day and tried to keep my mind on other things. This was a slow period at work, and I tried to stay occupied. The day seemed unusually long. I wondered how long I would have to wait for a response from Lee.

"By the time I got on the commuter train going home, I realized that my phone had not rung all day. I took a window seat in the Quiet Car. Before turning off my cell phone ringer, I checked for messages and there was Lee's office number. It had taken less than a day for my package to travel from the main post office in D.C. to Lee's office in Baltimore. Lee said she had received the package earlier that day, and everything was in order. She had called

Damon and given him my number, so I should expect a call from him."

I didn't receive a text back, but that was fine with me. It was an incredibly heavy moment for us both. She could have been overcome with her emotions, and simply not known what to write back. I mean, what does one say to that? "Yep, been a long time?" No. "Hey, how are you?" Um, no.

I sat on the bench trying to recall what I had just heard. "My name is Ann and I am your birthmother. Thank you for the beautiful letter you wrote to me…" I was so thankful she had heard me just as I'd wanted her to.

She said she had waited a long time for us to meet again, and she wanted to be in contact with me—but that she wanted our contact to be my decision. I pondered how hard it must have been for her, to wish for this moment for all the years since we parted.

She had reassured me that there were "no negative feelings or circumstances waiting to be revealed." That was comforting and put me at ease for the relationship we were blindly walking into.

Ann had shared that her own birthdate was September 24. As Lee read Ann's words, I was silently weeping. When I heard Ann's birth date, I stopped Lee immediately. "Wait! I'm sorry; are you saying her birthday is *tomorrow*?!"

"Yes, that's what her letter says," Lee answered softly. I was hearing my mother's words for the first time the day before her 63rd birthday! That was just incredible to me.

Shockingly, Ann revealed that she had attended Hampton University as well. Wow! We had attended the same historically black university a full 20 years apart from one another.

Who Am I Really?

She went on to say that she was a librarian for the federal government. I was astonished by that coincidence as I had just begun my job in federal service only three short months before. I figured if she worked for the government too, then she must work—and maybe live—nearby. *Cool*!

Ann expressed her gratitude to my mother and father for "giving me a home filled with love and a wonderful life." Those were the things she'd hoped for when we parted 36 years before, and I was fortunate to get her wish.

"I wanted to be found," she said. I was so glad, because I had really wanted to find her.

I had told Michele all about Ann's letter during our commute home together, so I was waiting patiently for her to return my text or call me. I was lucky that evening because our older children were both occupied with sports and activities away from the house. I was out on my deck grilling food for dinner and Michele had Seth inside.

Ann:

"Once I got home and started my evening routine, I realized the ringer on my cell phone was still in the off position. And there it was: a text message from a phone number I did not know. I opened it and the message simply said: '36 years.' Without hesitation, I dialed the number. I heard his voice for the first time, but I don't remember exactly what he said. I was in tears and the only thing I could say was 'I don't know what to say to you.' He laughed, and I laughed. The ice was broken, and the conversation flowed easily."

I stepped away from the grill and my phone for only a brief moment but, when I returned, I had a missed call and a voice mail. It was Ann. I listened to her message immediately, listening to her voice tremble as she introduced herself to me for the first time. Softly, nervously, she told me she didn't know what to say, but that I could call her any time of the day or night. She said she was on the verge of tears, but she was very happy. I really wish I had kept that very first message.

I called her back and she answered nervously. Her voice was gentle and sweet, filled with anticipation, burdened with anxiety. I don't really remember what we said, but I can remember a feeling of instant acceptance, connection, and rapport. I told her about how I had grown up in Columbia, MD, but after the HBCU tour I'd selected Hampton University. She told me that Hampton had been a bit of a tradition in our family, as her father and an uncle had also studied there. With a tinge of regret in her voice, Ann admitted that she had not graduated from HU.

Tuning to the fact that I spent my childhood in Columbia, Ann told me she'd lived in Laurel, MD, just a few miles away, during my teenage years. She said she had shopped at the Columbia Mall all the time; we couldn't help thinking that we had probably been there at the same time. Another amazing coincidence in our past.

Ann took a moment to reiterate the sentiments in her letter. She told me again that she had no secrets and I could ask her anything. Of course, I took the opening to ask about my birth father's identity. Ann shared the story of meeting a Detroit police officer named Mr. H, whom she never heard from again after she revealed her pregnancy to him. I had already decided I didn't want to find him, so I simply made a mental note of his identity and continued our conversation.

I asked Ann where she was living then, and she said she was back in Laurel again. She was only 30 minutes north of us in Silver Spring, Maryland. She was definitely close by, and the more we talked, the more I learned she had been nearby most of my life.

Curious about her employment as a federal librarian, I asked if she worked at the Library of Congress. It was the first library that came to my mind, and it was close to my office on Capitol Hill. "No, I work at the FAA," she said. I knew that was the Federal Aviation Administration in the Department of Transportation, but I had no clue where the building was downtown.

Calculating her route from Laurel to Washington, D.C. in my mind, I figured it had to be a long, miserable drive. I asked how she got to work every day, through the notorious congestion of D.C. rush-hour traffic. Ann said she took the MARC train from Laurel to D.C., then transferred to the D.C. Metro at Union Station for the ride to her office. "Oh, really? What's your metro stop?" I asked.

"L'Enfant Plaza," she replied.

"*Shut up! Me too!*" I exclaimed in utter disbelief. This woman went to my college, lived near me as a kid, and we share a metro station on our daily commute! What are the odds? Of course, I apologized for saying 'shut up.' Ann just laughed, because she understood what an amazing coincidence she had just revealed. She was incredulous too.

We talked about everything we could squeeze in, but there was just too much. We had lived a lifetime apart, and it was going to take time to get caught up. At the end of our call, I reassured her that it was OK to call me any time she felt like it. She said the same, and we were both so pleased that things had started off very well between us; it was a relief to feel so comfortable talking with each other.

Ann:

"We talked for more than an hour. When I hung up the phone, I had emerged from the darkness into the light."

I was so excited for this new beginning, Ann's warm reception, and all that there still was to learn about her—and therefore, about myself. I went upstairs to tell Michele everything I had experienced. Michele was in bed, where I interrupted whatever she was watching on TV to tell her the news. I calmly but excitedly told her how well our conversation had gone, and about the coincidences of our parallel lives. I said, "I think I'm going to surprise her at work tomorrow for her birthday!"

Michele, a naturally cautious person, asked, "Are you sure that's a good idea?"

"Of course, it is!" I exclaimed.

THE BIRTHDAY SURPRISE

I woke up the next morning excited for what that special day had in store. I knew that if things went well, it was going to be amazing. I got dressed in a chocolate brown suit, white shirt, and pink tie. (At the time, it was sharp.) I walked to the Silver Spring metro station, eagerly anticipating calling Ann. On the metro platform, with a huge smile on my face, I called and wished her a Happy Birthday. She giggled happily and said, "This is the best birthday gift I've ever had!" I was overjoyed to hear those words from her. We chit-chatted a bit before my train arrived, then I told her I had to go. I didn't want to be that guy yapping loudly on the train, and I didn't want to talk to her too long, or I might give away my plan to surprise her. She had no idea I was plotting to make her birthday far more memorable than a brief phone call.

I took the metro to Union Station, then trekked over to the Reserve Officers Association building on 1st Street for a conference. The Health Information Management Systems Society (HIMSS) was hosting the "Michigan Day on the Hill" event. Health information technology leadership from all over the state were in town to share their knowledge about how they were intelligently advancing IT utilization in healthcare for the benefit of patients. I was surprisingly captivated and attentive to the content of each speaker's remarks, given the grand plans I had to meet my biological mother in person later that day.

When the conference broke for lunch, I slipped out quietly and hailed a cab. It was a short drive to Ann's office at 5th Street and Maryland Avenue Southwest, so I just stared out the window at the bright blue, cloudless September sky, trying to relax and hoping for the best. When I got out of the cab, I just stopped for a moment to take in just how close Ann and I had been to one another since I took my new job. I looked to my right and stared at the entrance to the L'Enfant Plaza metro station, then looked left at the FAA building immediately across the street. "We both use that metro station, and her building is right there," I marveled to myself. I looked off into the distance in the direction of the HHS building where I worked, realizing my walk to that office would never be the same. I was in disbelief over our proximity to one another.

So many things could have gone very differently in each of our lives, preventing us from being that close to one another on our reunion day. If she had fallen in love with living abroad when she was younger, she could have been anywhere in the world when I decided to search for her. I might never have found her. If I had taken a different job after getting laid off, I might have worked anywhere else in the country, making our reunion logistically more challenging. But she was right there, only two blocks away from me in Washington, D.C.

I hoped deep down that I was truly prepared to make my first impression. The woman I was about to meet sent me off into the world 36 years before, prayed for all my successes in life, and hoped desperately for my return to her. And there I was, on her birthday. It was time to go meet Ann.

I walked into the FAA building, looking confident by outward appearances but feeling nervous. At the security desk, the guard asked in a robotic monotone voice who I was there to see. She asked hundreds of visitors the same questions every day, and I was no different than anyone else who had ever stood before her. "Ann Sullivan," I said.

"What's her phone number?" she asked, repeating a well-rehearsed line of questioning.

"Uh, I don't know. I've never met her before." I immediately overanalyzed my response, convinced she must have thought that was a weird thing to say. Only I knew what I was really there to do. I tried to smooth things over, so I clarified my innocuous response—making things worse.

"It might interest you to know that she's my biological mother, and I'm meeting her for the first time." The emotionless security guard suddenly brightened and engaged me directly, stirred from her boring routine with the news that something special was happening on her shift. Her eyes lit up; she smiled and asked me again for Ann's name, so she could look her up in the agency directory. The guard made a phone call and simply said, "There's a Mr. Davis here to see you." The guard suddenly gasped, wide-eyed, and hung up the phone.

Confused and concerned about her reaction, I asked, "Why did you gasp?"

The guard replied, "Because *she* gasped!"

In that moment, the reunification I set out to complete months before became a heart-pounding reality. It was about to happen. The guard pointed me to the elevators, gave me directions to Ann's office downstairs at the end of the hallway, smiled beautifully, and wished me luck. I was alone in the elevator; so, after the doors closed, I examined myself in their reflection. I straightened my tie and tugged at my suit, trying to make the best first impression I could. When the elevator stopped, the bell chimed, and the door opened. A short, light-skinned woman with rows of twisted hair was waiting to get on the elevator. We made eye contact and her jaw dropped open as she stared at me with shock. I knew instantly the woman was Ann Sullivan, and she recognized me from my pictures. In a flash, I saw my own face in hers. I took a huge step off the elevator and gave her an enormous hug, wrapping my arms around her shoulders and pulling her close. I was so overcome with emotion that my tears immediately flowed right onto her shoulder. I could barely muster a voice to whisper, "Happy birthday," in her ear. We stood by the elevators and cried together. We hugged so long that I was almost surprised to see her face for the second time when we separated.

Ann asked through her joyful tears, "What are you doing for lunch?"

"I'm here to see *you*!" I retorted. We laughed loudly and agreed to walk across the street to Au Bon Pain.

Standing in line together, we ordered our food, but I kept glancing over at her. She was shorter than me, and her hair was mostly grey after more than 60 years of life. But there she was. I bought her lunch and we sat in a corner near the windows and talked. I wish I could say that I hung on every word that came out of her mouth, but truthfully, I don't remember a single thing she said. I was too busy raptly staring at her face in sheer amazement, and thinking *Oh my god, I look just like you!*

When we left the restaurant, we stopped face to face for our first farewell. I could tell she was nervous, but I felt completely fulfilled and fairly relaxed. I reassured her, "We're good, you don't have to worry. You can call any time." She smiled hugely and hugged me to say thank you. I escorted her back to her office across the street, hugged her again, and said goodbye. My feet seemed to float above the ground as I walked back to my office.

I couldn't concentrate on work that afternoon. I was ecstatic and still stunned by what had just happened. I told my closest colleagues all about it through tears of joy. When I left for the day, I went back to L'Enfant metro station for the ride home. Standing on the train platform I felt this urge to shout, "Do you even know what happened to me today?!" I wanted to tell all others I saw, but as I looked into the faces of the other commuters, I could see that we all had things on our minds. I was overjoyed; others looked intense, even sad. I tried to imagine what they might be going through. Were they worried about their children, their parents, their jobs? In that moment, I recognized acutely that we all have a story to tell, and at different times in our lives the narrative changes. I kept my joy to myself, wishing I could spread it over everyone around.

In the following days, it became clear how fortunate we were to work so close to each other. We could get together at a moment's notice, and we often did. While I was sitting in meetings at work, I would look at my calendar to see where I had pockets of free time. I would shoot Ann a quick text message to see if she could meet me at Starbucks, halfway between us. She almost always did. We drank tons of coffee and ate many lunches; sometimes, we met twice in one day. I had so many questions, and she reassured me that I could ask anything I wanted. During one of our conversations, Ann admitted, "You found me at the right time. If you had found me earlier in my life, I would not have been ready. But now, I'm comfortable with who I am." Ann was open, very sweet, and we were comfortable around one another.

I've likened those early days in reunion to that warm feeling you have when you first fall in love with someone. You think about the other person constantly. You wonder what they're doing, and if they're thinking about you too. You can't wait to share things from the present, or random memories from the past. Obviously, the feeling was different, though, because it was the love between a mother and her son who had never known each other before.

For the first 30 days, we didn't make any further introductions to other people in our families. The moment was all about Ann and me. We were solidifying our bond; there would be plenty of time for the others to get to know us, after we had acquainted ourselves.

Two weeks after we reunited, we agreed it was time for Ann to meet Michele. I had been sharing details of our coffees and lunch dates with Michele, and she was supportive the whole way. She patiently gave us the time and space we needed to figure things out. She also worked in downtown Washington, D.C., so the three of us had a lunch date for their first meeting. I was looking forward to introducing them to one another, because unfortunately, Veronica and Michele didn't have a very good relationship. Veronica's mental deterioration had prevented her from accepting Michele in my life. Meeting Ann gave Michele a chance to build a new relationship, with a different mother-in-law. Thankfully, they got along very well.

Ann wrote in a card to Michele:

Dear Michele,

From the moment you introduced me as your mother-in-law, I have grown this special love for you. I saw you first through Damon's eyes when he talked about how you met and married. When lovers speak of their beloved, it touches the hearts of all in their presence.

I am so happy to be part of your beautiful family. Thank you for accepting me.

With
love, Ann

My 37th birthday was approaching rapidly, and it was exciting to think that it would be the first birthday that I would celebrate with Ann. Her 63rd birthday and our reunion day had been spectacular for both of us, but I didn't want her to feel like she had to do anything special for my birthday. I didn't want for anything, and I surely didn't think Ann should go out of her way to get me a gift. In the days leading up to October 14, I made sure to play down my birthday with her, naively thinking she would honor my wishes. "Listen, I'm all grown up now, so you don't have to get me anything for my birthday," I said, trying to relieve her of the pressure to buy me a gift.

She looked at me with mocking disbelief and sarcastically said, "I'm still your mother! I haven't seen you for 36 years, so you'll excuse me if I do what I want to do for you." I smirked at her, then looked down at my feet like a kid in trouble. I looked up with my eyes, jokingly said "sorry," and we laughed.

On Wednesday, October 14, 2009, Ann and I took a morning break to grab coffee. I waited for her on the corner of 3rd and C Street in between our offices, smiling as I watched her walk toward me with a large gift bag in hand. From a distance, I could see her smiling, which made me smile even more. She reached out and gave me a big hug when she arrived, grazing my back with the hard item in the gift bag. She kissed my cheek as she said, "Happy Birthday!" I could see she was really excited for us to be together. We walked to Starbucks, ordered our drinks, then then sat down to chat.

Ann shared that one of her passions had always been genealogy, and she had spent many hours over the years documenting the family's history. Trained as a librarian, she was perfectly suited to locate important information in archives and sift through heaps of evidence about our family. Proud of her diligent work, she told me she'd even found evidence that one of our distant relatives had fought in the Civil War, and that his name might be listed on the African-American Civil War Memorial. That was exciting to hear, and I knew exactly where the memorial was: on Vermont Ave. and U St., in northwest D.C. I drove past it often, commuting home with Michele. Then she reached in the bag and pulled out a huge purple album. The front cover had a slot for a featured picture, and in that space was a photo of us on our reunion day. I was moved to see that she had already incorporated a picture of us into my gift, but that small gesture was nothing compared to the artifacts contained within.

Who Am I Really?

On the first page Ann had written in perfect calligraphy *Ancestors and Relatives*, introducing me to what I was about to see. The second page blew me away. It was a full-page black and white group photo of Ann, standing next to her much taller friend Grace Thomas. It was the first picture I ever saw of Ann in her younger days, and she was absolutely beautiful. The way her hair was curled up at the ends and the frames of her glasses were quintessential styles of 1963. There were smaller photos of her throughout the years on the following pages. *Wayne State, 1971*, one photo's caption read, beneath a shot of her pointing defiantly into the camera, looking almost militant with a massive Afro. *Belle Isle, Detroit—You and me*, another hand-written caption read. She was leaning up against a statue, pregnant with me. *Ann, Adeline, & Bill, Aug. 25, 2001* described a shot of the siblings on their reunification day. It was unbelievable to get these glimpses into Ann's past as I flipped the pages and watched the decades go by.

I didn't think I could be moved any more by my gift, but flipping the pages further proved me wrong. I inherently knew what it meant that Ann was a genealogist and had documented our family's history, but it didn't register in my mind that she was sharing the story of her passion with me by gifting her years of work to me. The next section was called *Family Group Records*, and it was filled with genealogy tables. Each page had sections for detailed information about a family: mother and father names and birthdates; place and date of marriage; occupation; religion; and children's names, birthdates, and locations. I was reading the history of our lineage, dating back to the days of slavery in America. I even saw an entry for Edward Crapster, James Arthur Sullivan's grandfather, the Civil War veteran.

On Ann's personal family group record documenting herself in the family tree, she had listed one child, *Michael Anthony*, and footnoted the page. *This child was placed in adoption. His father was a police officer in Detroit, Michigan (the metropolitan police). His name would have been changed by the adoptive parents.* There I was, written into the family's history with as much detail as she knew. I gave Ann a huge hug and smiled widely at the amazing gift she had thoughtfully assembled: the knowledge of my maternal family history.

One month after our surprise birthday reunification, I asked Ann if she was ready to meet her grandson, Seth. She excitedly said, "Yes!" Then I reminded her that Seth would have to call her something, and we needed to think of her preferred grandmotherly name. She was visibly perplexed and excited. She was about to be introduced to my kids as their grandmother, and she needed an appropriate moniker.

"Grandma Ann," I suggested.

In an exuberant loud whisper of approval, she said "Oh! I like that!" We planned for her to meet our youngest son, her blood, at our home that weekend.

It was a sunny, crisp, and cool fall Saturday morning. I peered out the window periodically, anticipating Ann's visit. When she arrived, I watched her park her car, then walk up the steps of our townhouse. I noticed she was mumbling her inner thoughts to herself, with a slight smile of excitement about the little dude she was about to meet. Seth was almost two years old, adorable, and curious, which was perfect for engaging his grandmother for the first time. When I opened our front door, I called to Seth, "Come here, Buddy; it's time to meet Grandma Ann." He was too young to truly understand the gravity of what was about to happen. He toddled over to the front door, then hid behind my legs, too shy to come out and meet a new person.

Like any adult who recognizes a chance to win a kid over with a game of hide and seek, she bent over to her side and peeked around my legs, then said, "I see you back there!" He leaned further in the opposite direction, playfully trying to escape her gaze. But she quickly switched sides to see him again, and that was it. He thought she was fun, and soon they would be in love. My first biological relative, my son, was meeting the woman who had given me life. By finding her, I could connect her generation of our family with his. Connecting them meant almost as much to me as finding Ann for myself. My heart was full.

I also wanted to introduce her to my parents. My hope was for them to share gratitude with one another for everything each had done for me: Mom and Dad to Ann, for offering her boy into adoption; Ann to my mother and father for loving me as deeply as she hoped for. Sadly, Veronica's paranoid schizophrenia forbade such a meeting. I had finally come to terms with her mental illness, but I was still disappointed that it prevented one of my wishes from coming true. Thankfully Dad still had all of his faculties, and was supportive of my search and reunion.

Autumn was rolling along, and the days were getting shorter and colder. Dad invited everyone to his house, across the street from ours, for Thanksgiving dinner. Michele, our three kids, and I walked with Ann to my Dad's house for the preeminent time of year when Americans give thanks, and I had so much to be thankful for that I couldn't stop smiling. We laughed, told stories, and visited with each other individually, sharing the blessings of having family close and feeling love flowing throughout the house. I've had some excellent Thanksgiving holidays in the past, but that was one of the most meaningful; it epitomized what the holiday of giving thanks is about.

Ann shared my enthusiasm for introducing me to her family, so several months into our reunion, she arranged for me to meet her sister Adeline, as well as her niece Mary Ann and her family. It had only been Ann and myself connected to one another before; with each introduction my family grew around me, and it felt great.

Christmas was another milestone in our reunion. It was our very first one together, and I knew if it was anything like my birthday, Ann was going to do whatever she darn well pleased for me. So, I just kept my mouth shut. She came to our house on Christmas day, toting a small gift bag in her hand, which she handed to me as she entered. She simply said, "You can open this later." I was already thankful for whatever she had brought, so I respected her suggestion and rested my gift on the table near the front door. We enjoyed some great family time and had another wonderful meal, then Ann left to go home. We were both fulfilled from an amazing day with our family.

Later that evening, I picked up the gift bag as I passed by, then I sat down by myself in the living room to open it. There was a small bundle of plain off-white tissue paper, and a small greeting card in an envelope. Still a kid at heart, I skipped the card and went straight for the gift. The tissue paper bundle contained eight flat, circular glass holiday ornaments that were exact replicas of each other. They had a raised snowflake design in the center, and the year 1973 etched underneath. I opened the envelope to read the hand-written message.

Dec. 21, 2009

Dearest Damon,

At Christmas time in 1972 I believed that it might have been possible for us to be together in 1973. I wanted to start a new family tradition. I bought these snowflake Christmas ornaments with the intent to put them on our tree in 1973. But as I have told you, I could not break the bond that had already formed with your new family. Since 1973, I have hung these snowflakes on my tree. (Except 1985, when my mother died.) I am overjoyed to pass them on to you, except for one!

Love Always,

Ann

I cried. I was stunned that Ann had kept the ornaments I was holding in my hands for my whole life. I couldn't believe any gift could be so thoughtful, so patient in its curation. Tears of joy streamed down my face again. Ann's Christmas gift to me had been 37 years in the making.

When I called to thank Ann for such a wonderful gift, she shared more of the story behind the ornaments. She admitted to me, as she had in her introductory letter, that she'd known my parents and I were bonding more deeply with each passing day. She had forced herself to live with her decision to let our reunification be my decision. She told me she'd researched the process for locating relinquished children and obtained the paperwork to launch the process, but she couldn't bring herself to submit it.

In June 2010, I was on business travel in Detroit, MI. My boss, Dr. David Blumenthal, was making a big announcement regarding the advancement of health IT via grants from the federal government. I was the point man coordinating his time on the ground and I wanted things to go well, so I was very busy in D.C. in the days before our departure. At first, things weren't going great. The city was suffering in the midst of an economic downturn, and I had booked my boss a room in a hotel that was gasping for its last breath. I needed his announcement to go well, and it did. Watching a healthcare leader of Dr. Blumenthal's stature deliver the good news that Michigan's healthcare systems won additional federal funding was exhilarating. But my feelings were starting to run deeper than the announcement as a weird sensation overcame me. I felt an odd connection to the people in the room; their faces were so familiar. Then it hit me… They were the people I was with for HIMSS Michigan Day on the Hill, and l was with many of them in the moments before I covertly escaped to meet Ann for the first time! Not only was I with them that incredible day in Washington, D.C. but at that moment I was standing in Detroit, the city where I was conceived. I was so consumed with the importance of the grant announcement that it had been completely lost on me that I was traveling to the city where Ann got pregnant, until that moment. Suddenly, I was laughing to myself about the irony of everything I was feeling.

I ducked out of the grant announcement reception to call Ann and relay the crazy experience I just had. "Ann! Guess where I am?!" I said, through a huge smile.

"I don't know where you are, Damon," she deadpanned.

"I'm in Detroit," I said, waiting expectantly for her reply. But the phone was silent.

"Hello?" I checked to see if we were still connected.

"I gotta go," she replied, then hung up.

I had spoken with Ann every single day since our reunion, but after that phone call we didn't talk for two days. I decided it was time to check in, so I called to ask if she was OK. She apologized for how she had behaved and explained that after she got pregnant and fled Detroit, she had avoided the city at all costs. She never went back there for her grad school graduation, and she'd even avoided connecting flights that touched down there. She said when I revealed I was there, she had no idea why and she was petrified that I would see someone I felt I was related to. In turn, I explained my need to call her from Detroit, because of my odd feeling of attachment to the people in the room. She told me she understood, and my explanation set her at ease. We were just fine thereafter.

Like many adoptees in reunion, I wanted to hear more about Ann's life before I found her. I wanted to hear what her childhood was like, stories from experiences she had during her travels overseas, and her thoughts and feelings along the journey of her life. She suggested we take a trip to her home town, Princess Ann, Maryland, so I could see where she grew up. In the summer of 2010 Ann, Addie, Michele, Seth, and I piled into Ann's Ford Edge, and I drove us to University of Maryland Eastern Shore. During the drive, I told everyone how I nearly applied to attend UMES.

When we arrived, it was clear the campus had changed and grown dramatically during the years Ann and Addie had been away. We drove up and down the campus streets as the sisters told stories from their childhood. Pointing down one road in the back of the campus, Ann said there were days when she and Addie walked up the dirt road together, and they could hear their father whistling loudly in the woodshop as he worked. (Seth hates my piercing whistling, but Ann loved it.)

On another less stressful work trip, I was headed to Chicago. Before my flight, I was sure to forewarn Ann where I was going, because I didn't want a repeat of the Detroit incident. She reminded me that her brother Bill lived in the Windy City, so I asked her to put me in touch with him. I built a significant break into my trip itinerary so that I could grab a taxi to the south side of the city. When I knocked on their door, Uncle Bill and his wife Chris welcomed me into their home, where we sat at his dining room table and talked.

Bill shared the story of his reunification with Ann and Addie, nearly 10 years earlier. He showed me pictures of his grandfather, James Edward Sullivan, whom I had never seen before. To my astonishment, he looked white and had a long face that resembled Abraham Lincoln's, without his iconic beard. Bill gave me a copy of the photo that I later added to the purple photo album Ann had gifted to me.

We exchanged information about ourselves and our pasts. He spoke with sad openness about his long-time status as an outcast from the family. I could see the burden in his eyes from how he was treated. I told Bill a little bit about myself, sharing with him that Michele and I adopted two children early in our marriage, and that Ann had a grandson. We talked for nearly two hours. Toward the end of our time, he paused to tell me I seemed like a good man. For my uncle, who came from his rough beginnings, to say that to me was high praise, and I truly appreciated his approval. Years later, Chris told me that my emergence and my occasional calls were very important to Bill. He was glad I was able to move forward with my life, and glad that we had connected.

In the years after I met Bill, he was diagnosed with pancreatic cancer. Three quarters of individuals diagnosed with pancreatic cancer die within the first year after diagnosis. The prognosis was grim, and he was in and out of the hospital during the final year of his life. Ann and I hatched a plan with Chris to surprise Bill together in Chicago, in December of 2012. Originally, we'd planned to visit him in the hospital—but as luck would have it, Bill was released just days before our arrival. When Ann and I knocked on Bill and Chris's door, Chris answered and ushered us quickly and quietly to their living room. "Bill!" she shouted through the house, "come here for a minute, but go through the kitchen to the living room." She was guiding his path with that suspicious prescription to make sure that he saw Ann and me together, at one time.

Draped in a quilt to keep himself warm, frail and slow, Bill shuffled his feet through the kitchen. He passed the dining room table where he and I had bonded, rounded the corner, and lifted his gaze onto two unexpected guests. He couldn't hide his bewilderment at the pair before him. It was as if I could hear his thoughts as I read his facial expressions. *What is Ann doing here? Wait, what's Damon doing here? Oh, my goodness; they're here together.* His jaw dropped open, then he smiled with welling eyes. Ann and I smiled uncontrollably, and our eyes welled with tears as we hugged Bill tightly. Soon after, Bill's kids Marla, Bill, and Kelly all came over to see their Aunt Ann, meet me for the first time, and share in the joy of our family being together.

That trip to Chicago was a special memory. It was the only time Ann and I traveled together, and I'm so glad that we did. Bill Owens died in September of 2013. He was 82 years old.

CHAPTER 11

The End of Five Incredible Years in Reunion

BEFORE I FOUND ANN, she was counting down the days to her retirement, after 29 years of public service, and busy planning her new beginning. Her long-awaited last day of work came at the end of 2013. Following her spirituality, she decided to move to Santa Fe, New Mexico. Ann had rented apartments everywhere she'd lived her whole life, but at that moment she decided that for the first time, she wanted to buy a house to call her own. She scaled back her belongings to the bare minimum to make her move as effortless as possible. Ann packed her Ford Edge and a U-Haul trailer with what little she had left in her apartment, and her friend drove her car to her new home. She moved to Santa Fe on December 13, 2013. People asked me why, when we'd just found one another, would she move away? I reminded everyone that Ann was following a spiritual path; she was excited to relocate in retirement, and I reassured them that there were plenty of flights to and from New Mexico. I was actually looking forward to having a cool new place to visit.

Ann settled in to her new house, and we talked every few days about her progress. I was excited to see her new home, so Michele, Seth, and I flew out for a long weekend in May 2014. We had a lot of fun meeting her friends and touring old-town Santa Fe. In one of the local art shops, Ann and I marveled at a beautiful turquoise and purple glass bowl that was marked down for quick sale. When we left, I tricked Ann into hanging out with Michele and Seth while I snuck back to buy the bowl as a housewarming present. When we got home, I placed it covertly on the dining room table. Ann walk past the beautiful piece several times without noticing. Michele and I caught eyes and chuckled a little, watching her. When she finally stopped in her tracks, Ann was surprised and overjoyed by our thoughtfulness.

Things were definitely different, having Ann so far away. We had gone from seeing one another almost daily to phone calls and periodic video chats. I was glad she was happy, but I missed having her close by. Later that summer, she expressed some concerns about her health. She told me she was "going through something," but she wasn't able to articulate exactly what was going on. When I asked her to elaborate, she explained that she was experiencing memory losses from time to time. She said sometimes she would completely forget her thoughts, or what she was saying to someone. She recounted an instance when she entered the post office but completely forgot why she was there. Her friend had to coax her onward to go mail her envelope. She was drawing blanks, and it concerned her enough to tell me. Telling her story on the phone, she went silent mid-sentence. "See, I just did it," she said a moment later, with obvious concern. I told Ann she needed to see her doctor, and that I wanted to hear promptly what they said.

On September 13, 2014, Michele, Seth, and I were in Richmond, Virginia for the weekend visiting family. Michele's father was visiting, so we went out for a big family dinner at Maggiano's Italian restaurant at Short Pump Mall. Relaxing and chatting with everyone, my phone rang from a telephone number I didn't recognize. The call's location read as *Santa Fe, New Mexico*. Ann was the only person I knew in Santa Fe, so if she wasn't calling me herself, then I was about to receive some bad news about her. I stepped outside and tried to remain calm.

The caller told me her name was Adara, she was with another woman named Mari, and they were friends of Ann's. They explained they hadn't heard from Ann for several days, which was highly unusual, and they were worried. Each woman had called Ann's phone and knocked on her front door, but she hadn't answered. They had agreed to meet at her house, where they recruited Ann's neighbor to force her front door open. Inside, they had found Ann, deceased on her bathroom floor. My eyes burned and tears streamed uncontrollably down my face as I sobbed. The woman who had brought me into this world, trusted another set of parents to raise me, and hoped I would return to her one day was gone. It was too soon; we had so much more life to live together! She had just started a new chapter of her life in Santa Fe, and she had only purchased her home nine months prior. We were only 16 days short of the five-year anniversary of our reunification, and her 68th birthday. But I would never see Ann Sullivan again.

On Wednesday, September 17, Michele, and I flew to New Mexico to begin the process of managing Ann's affairs and packing up her belongings. It was really sad that the reason for our second trip to Santa Fe was because Ann was gone. Her lovely friend Mari picked us up from Albuquerque International Sunport airport, and drove us straight to Riverside Funeral Home there in the city. The funeral director, Danielle, expressed her condolences for our loss, then walked us through the process and options for memorializing Ann. I knew for sure Ann wanted to be cremated, but since I didn't have her official Last Will and Testament, I didn't truly understand all of her final wishes. We were making tentative plans for which we had no concrete guidance. We wanted to verify Ann hadn't left any guidance we weren't privy to before solidifying memorial plans, so we agreed we had to get to her house to try to find a will, if one existed.

Who Am I Really?

We left Albuquerque, arriving at Ann's home in Santa Fe about an hour later. Mari told me gently that she had cleaned up the bathroom a little, so I wouldn't have to see it the way it was when Ann passed. I thanked her, then left her and Michele in the car while I took a moment to enter Ann's home by myself. It was my second time ever being in her house. I went to every single room in the house, taking my time, before going to Ann's bedroom. I was preparing myself to see the place where she took her last breath.

My understanding was that Ann had gotten out of bed to use the restroom on Thursday night when she suffered a hemorrhagic stroke. When I entered her bedroom, I could see that her bed had been slept in. Her sheet, white with tiny purple flowers, was tossed over to one side with the light blanket, and I could still see the twists and wrinkles of her fitted sheet where she'd left her bed for the last time. I sat down on her bed where it looked like she had gotten up. I could see the bathroom floor, where an amazing life had ended. I took my time and let the tears flow down my face, trying to accept the tremendous loss.

After several minutes alone, I composed myself and wiped my eyes. Then I went back outside to let Mari and Michele know my moment was over, and I was ready to get to work. We went into Ann's closets and drawers, pulling out everything we could find that might have important papers in it. Michele was amazing at locating, categorizing, and bringing order to the array of documents. Mari carefully packed Ann's personal effects, found places to donate other items, and helped us think strategically about our next steps.

Michele left very early Friday morning to get home to Seth. I drove her to the airport in Ann's car; right after her plane left, my cousin Mary Ann's plane landed. We hugged one another tightly when I picked her up curbside. Mary Ann had traveled alone, leaving her husband, children, and her frail mother back in Baltimore. We drove to the funeral home to meet Danielle again. We discussed the plan for Ann's cremation, and agreed she would have liked having her ashes infused into blown art glass mementos.

We drove back to Santa Fe, talking the whole way about our beloved Ann. Since I'd only known her for five years, nearly everything Mary Ann had to say about their decades together was news to me. She told me how Adeline had moved to Kentucky to care for her own mother when Mary Ann was 19, around the same time Ann returned to Baltimore. She and Ann grew to be very close, almost like sisters. It was suddenly more obvious how devastating losing Ann truly was for her.

Later that same day, Pat flew in from Los Angeles. Ann's primary supporter when she was pregnant, and for countless other life moments I will never know of, had arrived to help one final time.

There was a lot of activity at the house when we arrived. Mari, an efficient property manager among other skills, had arranged for a contractor's estimate on new wood floors, a home improvement project Ann was planning. But it was Mary Ann's first visit to Ann's home, so Mari and the flooring contractor gave us some time alone. I walked Mary Ann around the house, much the same way I had done by myself, taking our time getting to Ann's room. I quietly let her take it all in. Her emotions flowed when she entered the master bedroom and felt the weight of the space. We gave each other another huge hug, shed a few tears together, then gathered ourselves to resume the business of sifting through documents and packing.

Sunday, September 21, we all gathered at the house one last time. I changed the locks, parked Ann's car in the garage, and closed up the house. Mary Ann and I went into the bedroom again. The bed was stripped down to the mattress and box springs. We sat there looking down at the bathroom floor in silence. After a few minutes, I got up and touched the bed where she had last been alive, walked into the bathroom and kissed my fingertips, then touched the floor where she died. I said "Goodbye," and left Mary Ann to do her own thing.

Searching through Ann's belongings, we were lucky enough to find a short, handwritten note where she affirmed her desire to be cremated, dictating that her ashes were not to be kept. We thought about her last request as we drove to Albuquerque. Pat drove Mary Ann and me to the funeral home, where Danielle signed over Ann's cremains to me and handed me a box. I was holding all that remained of Ann's physical existence, incinerated to fine dusty ash.

At some point, it hit me that considering where to spread a person's ashes was very different from buying a burial plot. The latter requires selecting a cemetery, entering into a contract to secure a space, and paying for that resting place. Ann's request required us to think creatively about a meaningful and appropriate place to spread her ashes. We were making an emotional investment in a place we would feel comfortable with.

Back in the car and on the road, we were very close to historic Route 66, just a few exits past the funeral home, so we exited the highway into the foothills. After a short drive, we found a serene spot for an impromptu ceremony. Parking safely on the shoulder, all of us then carefully walked through a cut between two hills, making our way through the brush. We wanted to get far enough off the road to share a private moment together. Using our phones, we all took pictures of our final moments with Ann. I opened the package of ashes carefully, then we took turns tossing her ashes into the light breeze, spreading them intentionally amongst the stones, or making a trail of ashes down the dry creek bed. Looking for places to spread her ashes had an odd light-heartedness mixed with intentionality. But when I reached into bag for the last handful of Ann's dusty cremains, I felt the sense of loss return. When it was gone, only memories would remain. I shed a final tear as I dropped the last bit of Ann Cecile Sullivan onto the ground in New Mexico.

We drove away with dusty hands and a few hours to kill before our flights departed. Naturally, we decided we needed food, and Mexican was on everyone's mind.

Back in Baltimore, we held a Celebration of Life service to remember Ann. I met so many of her friends from the Eastern Shore and various chapters of her life that day. Mary Ann and Adeline put together an incredible event that allowed us all come together on her behalf. I shared the following thoughts as my tribute to her life:

Celebrating Ann Cecile Sullivan
September 24, 1946–September 13, 2014

First, I want to sincerely thank everyone for gathering here today to celebrate the life of Ann Sullivan.

Who Am I Really?

It has been a fascinating experience to connect faces with the names of people Ann had mentioned to me, or were recently introduced to me under these circumstances.

Now, I want everyone to think for a minute:

Reflect on your children, if you have children, or think about any of the children you've ever been close to during your lifetime. Think about the feeling of deep emotional investment we have in our kids. We laud their successes as if they were our own personal achievements, and we can't help but take their failures personally on some level.

Now…imagine your life without that child.

If you're a mother, you may find this particularly difficult because your children came from your love, from your body, and you've been with them since the day they were born.

But Ann wasn't able to share the same experience.

When I was born in October of 1972, we were separated almost immediately because she had made one of the hardest life-changing decisions a person has to make when she asked herself this question: "Am I able to give this child the best possible life, or shall I trust other loving parents to raise my baby as their own?"

Right here in Baltimore, Maryland, with the help of her lifelong friends Pat Kiah and Sharon Holley, she had successfully hidden a full-term pregnancy from friends and loved ones in an elaborate scheme of deception. But that moment when she left the hospital, victorious in the fact that no one found out she was pregnant, she began a lifelong battle as to whether she had made the right decision to place me into adoption.

She began to hope that one day she would see her son, Michael Anthony Sullivan, again.

Try to imagine the days when she thought she had made the wrong decision, and she wanted more than anything to have her son back. She told herself that she would find a way to make things work, and maybe we'd be together by Christmas of 1973. So, she bought glass ornaments for the Christmas tree she hoped we'd share that next year that say "1973," to mark the year we were reunited.

But that (reunification) never came. With each passing day, the distance between us grew larger as the bond between me and my mother Veronica Anderson and my father Willie Davis strengthened.

And the years went by...

As with anyone's life, Ann's life had many chapters.

She was married, then divorced. She lived abroad in Germany and Spain, visited countries across Europe and Africa, and enjoyed life. She explored the world around her through the lens of her camera, or the study of her own spirituality.

Somehow, she found her way back to Baltimore, where she could be geographically closer to her niece Mary Ann and continue their deep bond.

Eventually Ann moved to Laurel, Maryland, just a few miles south of here. She had unknowingly settled mere minutes east of Columbia, Maryland, where her baby boy was growing up in a nurturing home with the very parents she'd hoped would love me as their own.

Living minutes from one other, we were still a lifetime apart.

Throughout her life, whenever she got really close to someone she trusted, she revealed to them that she had a son out there. But she had promised herself she would not look for me. She wouldn't disrupt my life and if I was happy, she would let it be so.

And the years went by...

Just try to imagine how she felt in 1986 when she watched the cinematic classic *The Color Purple* at the movie theater with a friend. Ann was riveted by the story of slavery and survival until the very end of the movie, when Whoopi Goldberg's character, Celie, is reunited with her children after 40 years apart. Suddenly, Celie's tears were Ann's tears, and the friend with whom she had gone to the movie theater was forced to leave her in her theater seat, inconsolably crying. Ann was overcome with the raw emotion of what she hoped that moment could feel like for her, when she reunited with me one day.

Just try to think of how it must have felt, if from time to time when you watched the news, you just had to hope that your son was not one of the young men returning to the safety of the United States as a wounded warrior: that a son you didn't know was healthy and happy, not injured or even killed in war.

It must have been a personal torture, not knowing anything. She was alone in the depths of a mother's worry. *Is he alive? Successful? Incarcerated? Who is he now? What could he be doing at this moment and is he safe?* I'm sure these questions ran through her mind, and many more.

In 2002, she decided she wanted to research how parents can reunite with children they've given up for adoption. Again, she talked herself out of breaking her own sacred vow to let me live my life.

Then one Friday night in September of 2009, she retrieved her mail to find a letter from the City of Baltimore. *That's odd*, she thought. *I haven't lived in Baltimore for years.*

She was incredulous that such a mistake could have been made, after so many years away from the city. Surely it must have been some mistake. But when she opened the letter, her heart soared. The letter was from Baltimore social services, and it read, *I have some important, updated information to share with you from a matter in 1972.*

The day she had longed for since October 14, 1972 had come; she was aware that I was looking for her.

She had waited 36 years to get some sign that I was looking for her. Unfortunately, she had to suffer through the entire weekend, overflowing with anticipation, in what amounted to a cruel irony. She couldn't call the office number for the social worker until Monday morning!

That Monday, her weekend of agonizing anticipation was finally satiated when my social worker, Lee Borris, read the letter I had written specially for her.

I spent hours crafting that letter, word by word. I wanted every single thing I said to be meaningful, because this was my one chance to make a first impression with the woman who brought me into this world.

"You must be filled with so much anticipation and emotion for what I have to say to you after 36 years," I began.

I took my time with my words, making sure I conveyed that I had grown up healthy and had turned out fine. I tried to reassure her that the decision she had made a lifetime ago was the right one, and that while I knew this was a very emotional moment for her, I would welcome a chance to connect with her when she was ready.

I had signed the letter, inserted photos of my wife Michele and me on our wedding day, and put in a picture of her grandson Seth as well, just in case my letter ever did find her.

Thankfully it had.

Just over a week later, I was at work when my mobile phone rang. The caller ID showed it was my social worker.

I knew she would only call if she had news. Yet somehow, I still couldn't believe that she'd found my biological mother in such a short time. Lee told me that Ann had received my letter, and she was ecstatic that I wanted to find her. I told Lee I would love to get a letter from Ann in return.

In another week, on September 23, 2009 Lee was on the phone again to say she had my letter from Ann, and she could read it to me or mail it.

Who Am I Really?

I told her I wanted to hear it, but I needed to get to a place where I could be alone. I raced out of my office and across the street to the Botanic Gardens, the location where the video clip many of you have seen was filmed.

I sat alone on the park bench where Lee's angelic voice read my mother's words to me, the first words I had ever heard from Ann. She told me she had waited a long time for this day.

Part of her opening read: "Your words were filled with sincerity, respect, comfort and concern for my feelings. It tells me a lot about the person that you are."

She went on to tell me details about herself, and her life. The letter read: "I was born September 24, 1946 in Kentucky but grew up in Maryland."

I immediately stopped Lee and said, "Wait, are you saying her birthday is tomorrow?!" It couldn't have been more serendipitous that I was hearing what amounted to my mother's voice the day before her birthday.

I sat on the bench in tears, overjoyed by the feeling of being connected to Ann by her own words. Lee told me things were now up to us. She would give Ann my phone number, and I could have Ann's; the rest was our decision.

At that moment, I wanted to call Ann immediately—but it was mid-afternoon on a workday, so I chose not to call her because I knew we would both melt into a puddle of tears, incapable of returning to our jobs.

So, I sent her a text message. "36 years..."

That could only be from me, and she would know right then that we were connected. She called me later that same evening, and we talked for what felt like hours. We had an instant rapport, and a connection that was undeniable.

I learned all kinds of things about her, where she had lived, and where she'd worked. I was astonished to learn that we had both attended Hampton University, and that Hampton was seemingly in the family blood.

I couldn't believe my ears when I learned we were both federal employees, getting off at the same metro stop. We worked only two blocks from one another!

I immediately decided to find her the next day, and surprise her for her birthday.

The following morning, I called to wish her happy birthday from the metro platform in Silver Spring as I made my way to work. She told me then that it was already the best birthday she'd ever had—but she had no idea what was to come.

At lunch, I left my meeting to head to her building. The guard in her building sent me downstairs, with instructions on how to get to Ann's office.

Descending in the elevator alone, I made all of the final adjustments for the best first impression I could make; I tugged at my suit jacket, this very suit, straightened my tie, and then the elevator door chimed. *Ding*!

The door opened and a woman stood in front of me, looking at my face with a mix of familiarity and shock. I could tell by the look on her face that she recognized me from my picture, and knew the woman before me must be Ann Sullivan.

I dove on her for a huge hug, as tears of joy streamed down both of our faces. We reunited on her birthday with a surprise visit that culminated in a moment that no one could have planned.

We had lunch together that day, but I don't remember a single word she said. I only recall staring into her face, thinking, *oh my god, I look just like you!*

When our lunch ended, I escorted her back to her office, where we took the picture you've all seen of the day we reconnected. Before we parted ways, I made sure to tell her, "We're good. Everything's OK, and you don't have to worry; you can call me any time."

In the coming days, we spoke to one another every day of the week, and saw each other almost as frequently. I would call or text when I had a few minutes open on my calendar, then we would meet at a Starbucks that was between our offices to catch up and learn more about one another.

I've likened that period after our initial reunification to that feeling you have when you first meet someone and you fall in love. When you're apart, you wonder what they're doing, what they're thinking about, and if they're thinking of you. When you're together your heart is warm, you're full of smiles, and they have your undivided attention as you cling to everything they say.

Today, when I immerse myself in the pages of that purple photo album she gave me when we first met, or I look through some of her old, very detailed, and informative genealogy notes and discoveries, I realize how important they are for my discovery of the family's history—*my* history.

I look at photos of Ann from years gone by and wonder who she was then. What she was thinking? How was she feeling? But now I can't ask her.

I want to express my deepest, most sincere, and heartfelt thanks to everyone in the Sullivan family who has welcomed me into their lives, like my cousin Mary Ann, her husband Franklyn, and their children Kyle and Kayla.

I especially want to thank Aunt Adeline, who recently told me how shocked she was so many years ago, when Ann revealed to her that she had given a baby up for adoption.

I also want to truly thank my own family. My mother, Veronica Anderson, who is unable to be here with us today, and my father, Willie Davis, who never hid my adoption from me, but allowed me to embrace it as part of who I am.

For as long as I can remember, they have always said they would support me if I chose to seek my biological parents. I'm so thankful for their strength in knowing that no matter what, I am always their son.

I want to thank my amazing wife Michele, who has been a source of strength and support in every way, and my children Seth, Sam, and Carissa, who have come to understand what it means for parents to adopt and love a child as their own in our home.

Thanks as well to all of Ann's friends who have known her so many more years than I did, and were so excited for her when we reunited.

Some of you have asked for readings from Ann's poems. I recently received an email from an old friend of hers, Phyllis Brown, who told me she thought Ann was "one of a kind and very special." Everyone I've heard from has expressed the same comforting sentiments about Ann. In her email, Phyllis shared that Ann had read a poem by Virginia Satir, then adapted it to represent sentiments from her own heart.

> I'll leave you with Ann's words:
> "I love you without clutching,
> appreciate you without judging,
> join you without invading,
> invite you without demanding,
> leave you without guilt,
> criticize you without blaming,
> and help you without insulting.

Who Am I Really?

This is what I bring to us."

Damon L. Davis, Baltimore, MD, November 1, 2014

http://www.slideshare.net/damonldavis/ann-cecile-sullivan-my-tribute

CHAPTER 12

SUDDENLY WILLIE DAVIS WAS GONE

THE EARLY PART OF 2015 was an interesting time in our lives. We had just returned from the annual Christmas trip to Los Angeles to see Michele's mother Susan, sister Stephanie, and stepfather Fred. Michele also had lots of travel on the horizon, including the Consumer Electronics Show in Las Vegas and the Grammy Awards back in Los Angeles. We were busy with our work lives, but there were far more important things on my mind at the time.

At 70 years old, Willie's health was declining. Over the years, he managed or overcame several life-threatening conditions, ranging from a quadruple bypass heart surgery in 1992 to his day-to-day hypertension and diabetes management regimens. Despite the health conditions he'd had to manage, he continued to live his life in ways that pleased him—even if some of his immediate joys were really long-term detriments, alcohol consumption principal among them.

In December 2015, I drove my father to MedStar Health to explore his options for a kidney transplant. His kidney function was declining again, so dialysis and transplantation were his only options. We both listened attentively to the medical staff as they briefed Dad and another older male patient on their options and opportunities for transplanted kidneys. It was an education for both of us. My guess is most people have a conceptual understanding of how organ donation works, but I doubt they have true clarity on the process behind the scenes. For example, I think most hope they'll be a direct match to donate an organ to their own loved one, as I had hoped to be for Dad. I imagined the two of us lying in parallel hospital beds as we prepared for a shared surgery experience.

In reality, most donors aren't a direct match for their intended organ recipient. Additionally, organ matches are intricately organized by their appropriateness for the recipient. The system tries not give a 20-year old's kidney to a 70-year-old patient, or vice versa. I also had no idea that a transplant candidate could register in multiple geographical areas to increase their chances of matching an available organ. We weren't limited to the Washington, D.C. area; Dad could have registered in Northern Virginia, Pennsylvania, and other areas. The organ donation process becomes a matrixed diagram of matching and organ exchange until an appropriate match is made. Donating my kidney might have meant it went into someone else in exchange for another person's kidney match, possibly through several other donor/recipient pairs, to be donated to Dad.

While we waited for Dad to be matched with an organ donor, his doctor asked him to make plans to start dialysis in early 2016. Traditional blood dialysis treatment is a life-altering process of being tethered to a machine several times a week, having one's blood extracted from the body and cleansed of waste, chemicals, and excess fluids, then returned to the body. Dialysis patients are often tired in the hours after the procedure, experiencing low blood pressure, nausea, and cramping, among other side effects. Dad wasn't looking forward to the adverse effect dialysis would have on his life. He was a tech and gadget guy, so he was really interested in the technological advances that allowed patients to dialyze at home overnight. He hoped he could maintain a full life during the day if he dialyzed while he slept.

Overall, we were optimistic but concerned. Dad was living alone after his third divorce, from Hazel, and I was a major part of his support network. I didn't worry about him too much when I was in town and could assist him easily. But I always worried more and felt guilty when I traveled without him.

The Grammy Awards, music's biggest night, was one of our favorites among Michele's work trips, partially because the trip took us to sunny southern California. Her career in the music industry lets her buy tickets to the big show, so she's attended for many years—except 2008, the year Seth was born. In February 2016 Michele, Seth, and I were in L.A. for Grammy weekend. We were staying at the W Hotel in Westwood, next to the campus of UCLA. Seth loves it there, and he usually has a great trip. It was a beautiful, sunny weekend on the West Coast.

On Monday February 15, 2016, Michele and I, her colleagues, and some of their spouses gathered in front of the hotel for the ride over to the show. It's an amazing festive experience to be inside the arena as the music industry mashes together performances by artists from different musical genres and time periods. The industry pays homage to artists who passed away in the prior year, and some of the most popular artists rock the stage with renditions of their latest hits in a theatrical mini-concert like no other.

We're lucky to attend the official Grammy after party next door, in the LA Convention Center. Thousands of people file out of the Staples Center dressed in black tie or music industry chic clothes and line up to enter the next show. Most people are starving for food and clamoring to get a cocktail after hours in our seats. Some of the women carry their high heels in their hands to give their feet a rest. The after party is a huge themed affair, decked from floor to ceiling with colorful decorations; imaginative, acrobatic dancers gyrate on mini stages, walk around on stilts, or swing on poles. Of course, there are more live musical performances on the main stage or in satellite rooms. It's like a musical circus. In any special event, I always try to remain humble and recognize that most people will never get the chance to do some of the amazing things we've done, but that year I was oddly disinterested. I didn't drink much; I kept my mouth shut and tried to behave, but I just wanted to leave.

In total, it's a long afternoon and night that traditionally ends with a trip to In-N-Out Burger in black tie before we retreat to our hotel rooms. Susan was watching over Seth as he slept in our room. She enjoys an evening at the hotel with her grandson, and we appreciate the free child care. Michele and I were exhausted when we arrived, and within a few minutes of sitting down, I passed out on the ottoman while the ladies chatted about the evening.

When I got up the next morning, I felt rested. We were flying back home that day; Michele was on a midday flight with her colleagues, Seth and I were on a later flight that afternoon. It worked out well, because Seth never wants to leave LA. Our later flight allowed him to have a huge pancake breakfast and one final swim in the pool.

I was poolside with Seth, taking in my last bit of L.A. sun and relaxation, while staying mindful that there was still a lot to do before we flew across the country. Seth needed to shower; he wanted one last run to In-N-Out Burger, then we had to navigate L.A. traffic in an Uber to make our flight on time. I checked my phone to see what time it was, so that I could give Seth his fair warning before he had to get out of the pool. But when I picked up my phone, I saw I had a missed call from Dad's best friend, Michael O'Bryant.

Mike never calls me, so I knew immediately there had to be something wrong with Dad. I tried to remain calm, but I didn't bother listening to the message; I called Mike back right away. When he answered, Mike said, "Damon, I just want you to know that I'm here for you. Seriously, whatever you need. I'm here for you."

I stopped Mike right there. "Mike, is there something you need to tell me?" Mike was silent for a moment, when he realized I had no clue what he was talking about.

"Oh, no; you don't know, do you?" he asked quietly. He had to hold back his own emotions, because the solemn duty of giving me the bad news had unexpectedly fallen on him. "Willie…died last night," he said apologetically.

"Oh, *no!*" I exclaimed. I immediately looked up to the sky, trying to keep my composure. Holding the phone to my ear, I spun quickly to look at Seth. My son was still playing happily in the pool, so I turned around, hoping he wouldn't detect my sorrow. I dreaded telling him that Pops was gone. I wondered how the hell I was going to make it on a cross-country flight alone with him, in the devastated state I expected to be in.

Mike told me all he knew about what had happened. Dad had been found on the floor of his apartment when he didn't show up to meet a buddy that night for drinks. I told Mike I was in L.A., and I would be home later that night. I thanked him for telling me about Dad and we hung up.

I looked to the sky again, trying to hold back tears and loudly whispering F-bombs to myself. They were filled with anger and sadness, and they were all I could do to prevent breaking down and crying. They were an aggressive outlet of emotion, stabilizing me before turning calmly toward my son. Somehow, being across the country put enough distance between myself and reality that I was able to keep it together.

I walked over to the edge of the pool, calling quietly to Seth to meet me at the pool's edge. I knelt down so I could be right next to his ear. "I have some bad news, Buddy." His little wet face looked up at me, sensing the seriousness of what I was about to say. "Pops died last night," I said, hoping he could keep it together. He said, "Oh, no," and I told him I was really sorry. I let him know we had 15 more minutes at the pool, then he had to shower so we could go get his food. I wanted to protect his little heart from the loss of his grandfather. They had grown so close as Seth grew up; I just wanted Seth to keep being my happy little boy.

I called Michele to tell her what happened. She was on the shuttle bus to LAX, preparing to board her return flight to the East Coast. She told me how sorry she was for our loss, and for not being next to me at such a sad time.

It was a long, sad flight back to the East Coast. When we got home, I immediately unpacked. I knew the rest of the week would be dedicated to the tasks and chores of closing out the odds and ends of my father's life. But first, I had to face the sad fact that my father was gone.

The next morning, Michele and I went to his apartment's rental office. They graciously extended their condolences, expressing how much they had liked Dad, and granted us the time we needed to vacate his home. We went upstairs to his front door, where I had another one of those moments when you realize the gravity of what you're about to experience. When you enter a person's home, the aroma reminds you of them; his apartment did so for me. But I could feel what had happened there, too. I could see the evidence of first responders who had tried to revive him. I could tell the coroner's office had wheeled the kitchen island away from the front door, giving themselves space to wheel his lifeless body away. Everything else was right where he left it, his apartment frozen in time. Dad's coat was on the tall chair next to the island, ready for him to pick it up as he headed back out the door. I could feel the void in his apartment and in my life.

In the following days, I learned the story of my father's final moments. He had borrowed his friend Darryl's car while he was out of town, so Dad drove to the airport to pick Darryl up. On their way home, they agreed to go out for a cocktail that evening. Darryl wanted to drop off his suitcase at home, so he dropped Willie at his apartment briefly, then returned to pick Dad up to head out for the night. I read the text message from Darryl on Dad's phone: "Hey, I'm outside." Dad had never typed a reply.

Family and friends sent condolences from all over the country and around the world. I received calls and emails expressing sadness, support, and love from Washington, D.C. to Sacramento, Saint Vincent and the Grenadines to Johannesburg. With my aunts, cousins, and several of Dad's close friends, we planned a celebration of Dad's life. He wouldn't have wanted us to be sad for our loss; Dad would have wanted us to be happy for the time he shared with us. We wanted every one of his dear friends, business associates, and social acquaintances to have a chance to gather and celebrate his life. Dad was known for his sharp, edgy style of dress and we wanted the people in the room to reflect his tastes. We agreed that everyone should don an outfit with some color, avoiding the solemn color black. Music played, hors d'oeuvres were served, and people from all points in Dad's life enjoyed reconnecting in his honor. Melanie Birch, the daughter of Dad's business partner Herb, gave the blessing. Herb Birch and Knowlton Atterbeary spoke on behalf of his friends. Michael O'Bryant Jr. spoke for the young people Dad had always tried to uplift, and I delivered the words of remembrance and love below.

A Celebration of Life for Willie H. Davis on February 27, 2016.

Willie Herman Davis

October 17, 1942–February 15, 2016

"He always had a smile." "He had my back." "He was my mentor." "He was so generous." "I looked up to him as more than just a good guy. His easy way with people and bringing together folks of all stripes, always struck me as a real talent, and a path for us all to take in the future." "It was good just knowing he was alive in this world." "I loved him so much."

Every one of these sentiments is true and could have come directly from my heart, but I want you to know that these are not my words; they are your own words, loved ones and friends. These are just a few of the many heartfelt messages I've received, read, and heard about my father Willie Davis.

But of all the things we can say about what he was to each of you, I'm the luckiest one, who can say he was my Dad.

We're all here because he made an impact on our world. He touched our hearts and lives with his humor, wisdom, and relentless search for a good time. We are family, friends, business colleagues, mentees, and drinking buddies. We have many reasons to be thankful to have ever known Willie Davis—but I won't lie to you, I do not count the hangovers we've all had because of him among them!

He was born in Tallulah, Louisiana in 1942, and raised in Kansas City, Kansas. His lifelong friend of 60 years, Waymon Guinn, told me that Dad was a very quiet guy in high school. I'm sure you all find that as hard to believe as I did! He says they were part of a club in their youth called the Flamingos, which was known for its members wearing suits to high school! Dad was always impeccably dressed. He was "clean," or "sharp as a tack," as they say.

Dad joined the U.S. Air Force, following his desire to see the world outside of Kansas City. In the Air Force, Dad was in medical administration, which was the basis for his extensive knowledge of health care. His duty stations during his four years took him to Puerto Rico and

March Air Force Base in California. The G.I. Bill helped him fund further education.

After his military service, he returned to Kansas City, where he worked for the Social Security Administration in a job at the GS-1 level, well beneath his qualifications. Good jobs were in short supply for men and women of African-American descent at the time.

He later went on to Rockhurst University, which was recruiting African-American students in the late 1960s. There, he earned his Bachelor of Science in Business Administration. As a hard-working student, dedicated to his own success, he attended classes in the mornings and his internship at Ford Motor Company in the afternoons.

He continued his studies later at University of Massachusetts, Amherst, where Dad got his Master of Business Administration.

Returning to Kansas City, he worked at the Black Economic Union, where he and Waymon, who had also joined the Air Force and attended Rockhurst with Dad, met Knowlton Atterbeary. All of them later went to work for Macro Systems here in Maryland, with Cluin Cameron and Herb Birch. Waymon told me that every one of those men went on to launch their own successful business.

Dad established the rest of his life here in Maryland. He married three times: to my mother, Veronica Anderson (who is not able to be with us here today), Libby Queen (who has also passed away), and Hazel Beach, who is with us here today.

I have so many hysterical memories of travels and adventures with my Dad.

When I was just a kid, he would take me to what used to be the Golden Flame restaurant here in Silver Spring, where he would hang out with the fellas: Al Naney, Michael O'Bryant, Mike's brother Klevin, Jim Schraf, Waymon, Knowlton, and many others. I, and many of the other kids of the fellas, would grow to regard these guys more as uncles than just Dad's friends. I would play Pac-Man for hours while Dad and the fellas socialized.

Once I heard him tell a woman there, "Oh, you like boats? I have a boat."

"You don't have a boat!" I blurted out with a child's innocent honesty. Guess who got a $20 bill to get more quarters for Pac-Man?

In Saint Vincent & the Grenadines, his friend and my father-in-law, Fredrick Ballantyne, would take us out for fishing trips. I remember one beautiful Caribbean afternoon we returned to port sailing west, marveling at an incredible sunset. In the warm glow of the setting sun, we clinked our beer bottles together and agreed, "It doesn't get any better than this."

One of Mike's favorite stories comes from the island of St. Martin on a family trip, where we all went to a seminude beach. Dad would pull out his camera and call out to us kids, "Hey! Smile!" as he blatantly snapped a picture of a naked woman over our shoulders. The photos later looked like we kids had photo-bombed the shot!

Another time in St. Martin, he and I were driving back to our hotel at a relatively early hour when we both paused, looked at each other, and asked, "Why are we leaving? We don't have a thing to do tomorrow!" We turned the car around and went back to the bar, where—of course—he saw someone he knew from the D.C. area.

I felt like everywhere we went he knew someone, and everyone I've talked to has said the same. I was astonished one year when we stopped to buy a Christmas tree, and he knew the guy selling the tree from another part of their lives. Dad's sister Shirley Gilbert once said, "D never met a stranger!"

Many of you know that I'm adopted, and that I was reunited with my biological mother, Ann Sullivan, a few years ago. She has since passed as well, but one of the best moments of my life was introducing her to

Dad, so that she could come face to face with, and say thank you to, the man who helped shape who I am today.

From time to time, people would tell Dad and me, "You guys look just alike!" I believe people saw some similarities in our physical appearance, but more likely, they felt a connection to the essence of who we are—and our genuine connection to and pride for one another.

Dad accomplished a great deal in his life. Birch & Davis Associates, Inc., the company that he, Herb, and their amazing team of colleagues and friends built, was known for both meticulous attention to corporate integrity and a congenial, fun atmosphere. Today, decades after the company was sold, I can still mention the name Birch & Davis and receive compliments about the great work everyone did as part of that successful organization.

However, one of Dad's proudest moments came when my wife Michele gave birth to our son Seth, now eight years old. His birth marked the first time I had ever known a blood relative. Like any proud father, I began reaching out to family and friends with the good news, and Dad was my first call. I could hear his smile when he congratulated us over the phone.

It felt like mere minutes after I had hung up the phone with Dad when a nurse peeked her head into Michele's recovery room and declared with some confusion, "Um, someone's Dad is here…" Ecstatic about his grandson's arrival, Dad had dropped everything and rushed to the hospital to see him! He loved and adored Seth, but he didn't want the usual *Grandad* moniker. He and I agreed we wanted a cool name for Seth to call him. So, we decided that the name his old friend Preston used for his Dad, Pops, was just right.

Dad shared the same energy and enthusiasm he had for Seth with literally every child he met. He *loved* babies and kids. He would make the craziest noises and faces to make any baby smile, and if they did, he would melt with joy.

Who Am I Really?

That love for children was fed by his involvement as a founding member and the vice chair of the Lee Montessori Public Charter School Board of Directors. He loved being part of a school dedicated to the advancement of as many young people as the talented staff have the energy and resources to support. I'm grateful to the school for the fulfillment that his involvement with your team gave him. I can say definitively that he would have absolutely loved the honor of having his name on the playground that you'll dedicate in his honor later this year. It means more to me than you know.

He was a boisterous, social man on the outside, and a warm-hearted sensitive man on the inside. He told me recently that he had befriended a homeless man along his local travels. After talking with this man, he discovered they shared an affinity for reading some of the same authors. So, Dad gave him his old books, and would occasionally buy the new ones for him when they came out. He was generous beyond compare.

I've heard from many of you how about how proud Dad was of me, and that message always warms my heart. No matter how old I get, parental approval and appreciation for the man I've become is an unparalleled mark of my success in life. So, as his spirit now flies, I go forward knowing I had his love—and I'm telling you, so did all of you.

You may know that Dad was a die-hard Kansas City Chiefs and Washington Wizards fan. In sports, an athlete's best effort is described as "leaving it all on the field," which is how Dad lived his life: to the fullest, leaving his best work instilled in all of us. There wasn't a friend he didn't love, a young person he wouldn't mentor, a small business he wouldn't support, or one last drink he wouldn't have.

What's left of Dad now is the afterglow of the brightest, warmest light many of us have ever known. I ask that you go forth with that glow in your hearts, and that we all treat one another and the people we meet with love and respect in Dad's memory.

Please join me in a toast to the life of my Dad, Willie Davis!

After Dad's body was cremated, my cousin Tanya suggested we should check to see if his Air Force service made him eligible for military funeral services. On Thursday, May 5, 2016, Arlington National Cemetery conducted a formal military funeral ceremony in honor of Private First-Class Willie H. Davis. Young military service men and women, who must have been about the age dad and Waymon were when they enlisted in the USAF, stood at attention and delivered the multiple gun salute. The military personnel presented me with the flag they had silently and meticulously folded into a triangle over the ash-filled urn during the ceremony. We took a short walk across York Drive to the columbarium, where I stood in front of the huge wall, holding my father's remains in my arms for the last time. I passed the urn up the ladder to the cemetery worker, who carefully placed it inside the small rectangular vault. He adjusted the urn to stand front and center, making sure the name tag on the front was facing forward. When he screwed the face plate onto Dad's spot in the columbarium wall, it was over. I stood there for a while, just looking up at Dad's final resting place. I turned around and saw Seth was standing beside me. His little arms were holding the folded flag, his grandfather's flag.

CHAPTER 13

The Mistaken Identification of Mr. H

Thankfully, in the wake of Ann's passing, my grief subsided. I focused on how fortunate I was to meet her and thank her for giving me life. I reminisced on and treasured the stories she'd told me about her own life. But it really started to hit me that conceiving me had taken two people, and I had only met one of them. Ann left this world in 2014, so it couldn't hurt her anymore if I sought answers about the identity of my biological father. My curiosity about the other half of my genetic equation grew stronger, and I felt free to enter the next phase of my journey.

While I wasn't adamant about locating the man, periodically I did web searches to see what I could learn about anyone with Mr. H's name. In December 2013, I started spending more time online, hunting for clues as to who this man could be. There were hundreds of Mr. H's online, all over the country. It was impossible to determine who he could be among the endless list of online profile links. In desperation, I switched to looking at Google Images of the men. If I could see a picture of this dude, perhaps I would see something of myself in him, and it could be a lead. But the pictures were no help either. Some of the men were black, others were white—but I didn't look like any of them. I gave up for a while, so I could gather my thoughts and launch a more intelligent internet search than these half-cocked shots in the dark.

I listed the things I knew about him from what Ann had shared with me. The fact that he was a Detroit Police Officer at the time of their relationship was an important clue. Was he still in Detroit? Maybe there were public documents online showing his law enforcement service to the community. I was feeling more confident that a new search based on the facts I'd gleaned from Ann's story would have positive results.

Reinitiating my search, I got some hits. The former cop went on to serve the public in several capacities, running for public office and even establishing a short-lived candidacy for president of the United States in the 1990s. But still, there were no helpful pictures. Not one.

I concluded that if he were around Ann's age or older, it was hit or miss how strong his digital presence would be online. Willie was a tech junkie who bought all of the latest gadgets, managed his own personally branded website, and had a significant social media presence. But I had no idea if this guy was as digitally available as Dad had been. I continued to search online sporadically over the course of months.

Eventually, I turned my attention to Ancestry.com. They were constantly adding public records to their database for users to browse. It's an amazing resource of information. I found census forms from the 1940s with names of his relatives, showing him as a child in his household. It had to be the guy, because his age at the time of my search would be about right. Next, I paid a few dollars for a PeopleSmart.com online records search to provide identifiable information. It was money well spent, because I got a few mailing addresses for him. My investigation was really starting to come together.

I decided to write an introductory letter to Mr. H, but it was a very different experience than the emotional outpouring I drafted to Ann. I was not writing to a woman whose body had given me life. I was writing to a man who didn't know I existed and might not be receptive to me interrupting his life with my sudden presence. I took the tack of brevity in my message, sticking to the facts as I knew them. But I didn't want my introduction to be too cold, either. I copied elements of my letter to Ann, conveying that I had a great life and I wasn't seeking anything from him. I hoped to put his mind at ease that I didn't require some special attention, making it clear that it was an open, honest introduction. I picked the two most current addresses from the People Smart report and sent the following introductory letter on January 6, 2015:

> Mr. H,
>
> In 2006, I had the incredibly good fortune to be reunited with my biological mother, Ann Sullivan, after 36 years as the product of a healthy and happy adoption. With our reunification, I was finally able to learn who my biological mother was, the circumstances leading to my adoption, and the name of my biological father, Mr. H.
>
> Ann told me my father was a Detroit policeman at the time of her brief acquaintance with him; therefore, it is my belief that you may be my biological father.
>
> I should tell you I've grown up healthy and very happy in Maryland. I'm 42 years old, I've been married for eleven years, and I have three children (two of whom are adopted). My parents have afforded me many opportunities to experience the joys of life, and my family gives me fulfillment beyond belief. So, you see, I have no agenda for establishing contact with you at this point in my life. This outreach is purely for the satisfaction of my own curiosity as to who you are.
>
> I'm sure by now you're filled with an indescribable series of emotions and questions. Please rest assured that I don't

wish to bring you or your family any stress with my appearance after all these years. However, I do want to offer you the opportunity to speak with me. Please take your time in deciding if you are ready to be in contact with me. Believe me when I say I harbor no ill feelings for the circumstances that brought me into this world; it's water long under the bridge by now.

If you should decide there is no reason to be in contact with me, I will respect your decision. However, you will certainly miss out on knowing the man that I've become.

Respectfully,

Damon L. Davis

I felt a different nervousness about this letter than I had with my introductory letter to Ann. My main concern was I didn't actually know his correct address; there was a chance my letter could have reached one of his family members before reaching him. I wanted him to have the chance to digest the information I fed him and process it for himself. I certainly did not want to rock the boat for the rest of his family. That's a common feeling among adoptees reaching out to birth relatives, especially if we suspect our lives will be a surprise to them. We don't want to disrupt the lives of others—but we are here, and we deserve to be heard.

A few days later, one of the letters I received appeared back in my mailbox unopened. I was a little disappointed to be holding my own envelope again, but I quickly realized only one letter had been sent back; the other letter was still out there. I was hopeful that it would find someone who knew Mr. H, and could deliver the news that I was looking for him.

Another week went by, but the second letter was never returned. One day, my phone rang from a Detroit phone number. When I answered, a man with a booming voice asked to speak to Mr. Davis, announcing himself as Mr. H. He said my letter had reached him at the church where he was pastor. I was immediately uneasy with the overbearing tone and cadence of his speech, especially for a first call between a possibly long-lost father and son.

I could barely get a word in during that first conversation as he continued to talk about himself. Nearly every sentence he spoke ended with praise for his personal savior Jesus Christ. My parents grew up going to church in Kansas and Missouri, but there was no church for me in my youth in Maryland. I know they raised me with the positive lessons they learned from their faith and church attendance, but I was always thankful that I was left to decide for myself what my own beliefs would be. Regardless of his zealotry, his vocal soaring and impenetrable conversation were not something I was used to in personal conversations. This guy was rubbing me the wrong way.

I asked him a few questions about himself, searching for clues about our connection to one another. He responded to a few of my inquiries, then suggested he could send one of his press packages by mail. He said it had a great deal of information and it would be a good way for me to get familiar with him. I hung up the phone feeling almost relieved that the conversation was over, and somewhat glad that he was in Detroit where it would be harder for us to connect. Before he ever called me, I had prepared myself for the fact that if I ever found this guy, it was unlikely to be as amazing an experience as I'd had when finding Ann. My very first conversation with Mr. H proved I was right.

However, I did feel a sense of achievement. Simply finding my biological father was a major goal in my journey to understand my paternal identity. I could check the box on that task, and just wait to see where things went from there. I didn't feel any pressure at all to force our relationship forward.

Who Am I Really?

A week later, a thick letter-sized package arrived in the mail. It was exciting to have this guy willingly sharing his history with me. To the left of the return address on the envelope was a paper cross that had been cut out and taped to the envelope. Another cutout piece of paper read *Jesus, King of Kings*. A third taped piece of paper, again, in the return address area, read, *God Our Father, Jesus Our Lord, Rev. 'Mr. H', Pastor*. Beneath the series of taped pieces of paper was a handwritten return address. In its entirety, the return address section of the envelope looked like a grade school collage about religion. I noted that not even the return address section of a piece of mail could leave his hands without a proclamation for the greatness of his savior.

I opened the envelope to find Mr. H.'s adult professional life well documented in an extensive series of photocopied artifacts, chronicling his life before I found him. There was a newspaper clipping highlighting his election to the Detroit Free Press Annual Prep High School All City Basketball team. Another paper chronicled his meritorious citation as a patrolman in the Detroit Police Department in the late 1960s. Other pages had extremely grainy black and white photos of him coaching youth basketball teams in the 1970s and '80s. One sheet listed all of his employment, from his service in the U.S. Army in 1960 to his work with Chrysler Corporation, many years later. In 1984, his political aspirations were made official when he was elected as precinct delegate. In the years that followed, he was a repetitive candidate for Michigan's congress.

In 1992, he was even a candidate for President of the United States, in a field of candidates including Ross Perot, George H. W. Bush, and Bill Clinton. Also included was an interesting letter from *The Montel Williams Show* saying they were considering producing an episode with the unheard presidential candidates, those generally left out of national media coverage.

His personal history gave the impression that he was a civic-minded community leader seeking to affect change. I found myself feeling both proud that I had come from his lineage, and saddened that I felt no connection to him whatsoever when we talked. As interesting as he appeared on paper, I still wasn't that excited to get to know him.

A few days later, he called again. I liked that he felt comfortable reaching out to call me, and it wasn't just me, the needy adoptee looking for answers, who was reaching out to him. We barely got past the opening exchange of pleasantries when he declared that he was renting a recreational vehicle to drive across the country to see me. *Wait, what*?! We had barely known one another a week, and I hadn't extended an invitation for a visit. This guy simply announced that he was coming! I immediately had nightmarish visions of the movie *National Lampoon's Christmas Vacation*, when Cousin Eddie (Randy Quaid) parks his RV in front of the Griswolds' house and empties the septic tank into the community sewer while standing in the street in his robe. There was just no way a road trip could end well, when I was already imagining worst-case scenarios. I decided I had to keep my composure, wait him out, and see if the plan came up again for discussion. Thankfully, it never did.

On another occasion within those first few weeks, he called again. The pattern remained the same: We briefly exchanged pleasantries, then he launched into a wild declaration. "I'm going to send you my resume. I'd take a job in security. I used to be a police officer for many years." I was incredulous. I'm thinking, *Hey! Man, you didn't even know I existed a minute ago, and now you're asking me to help you get a job?!* This connection wasn't going well for me at all.

Finally, in what would be our final conversation for a long time, I asked Mr. H about his memory of Ann. This man had been with my birth mother, and I was curious to know what recollections he had of their relationship and that period in their lives. In Ann's version of our story, she and Mr. H met, and they started to date. I wondered what his memories were of those days. Without hesitation or apology, he said, "I don't remember your mother." I tried not to reveal what a letdown it had been to hear those words from him. I felt like even if he hadn't remembered Ann, he could have said so more tactfully. It wasn't a cold delivery, it was just very matter of fact, lacking any emotional sensitivity for how I might receive his words. I felt like my birth mother, whom I had grown to love as a beautiful person, had been heaped on a pile of indistinguishable sexual conquests from his younger days. I knew in that moment that as I'd predicted before I connected with him, I wasn't going to get anything resembling the warm reunion I'd had with Ann. After our fairytale reunification, I'd always told myself, "There's nowhere to go but down from here." I just knew that our story had unfolded so incredibly that whatever happened next was likely to pale in comparison—and I nailed it, unfortunately. I decided I needed to let my contact with Mr. H lapse, and allow what little relationship we had to fade away. Locating and connecting with him had been enough; there was no reason to push things any further.

In April 2017, we were packing for another trip to Saint Vincent and the Grenadines. I had just launched the *Who Am I Really*? podcast, in which other adoptees share their journeys through adoption and their attempts at reunification with their biological family members. I had a sense of contributing to the adoption community through the podcast. Then it hit me that my own reunification experience was not complete. I had never actually met my biological father. The more I thought about it, the more it struck me that he was getting older and if he passed away, I would never have met the man that contributed to my existence. The road had been rough, but I decided I would have to suck it up, because I wanted to meet Mr. H.

I sent him a text and simply said that I was interested in meeting him. He called me back within a few minutes and asked me some very intelligent questions, making some good points. Among them, he asked if I had I seen my original birth certificate and seen his name on it. I had not; Maryland is a state where adoption records were sealed in 1972, and there was a good chance his name wasn't on my birth certificate anyway. It is my understanding that under certain circumstances, the birth mother is not required to name a birth father.

Secondly, he suggested that we submit samples for a DNA test to confirm our connection. It was a good idea, and I was glad the idea had been his and not mine. It meant he was genuinely interested in the result, and I had not coerced him into doing the test. Ann and I also did DNA testing with 23andMe, but she and I didn't require the official genetic validation of our connection that Mr. H and I needed. Coincidentally, Michele, Seth, and I had recently submitted our samples to AncestryDNA, so that seemed like the best online platform to connect us all together when the tests were complete.

With each question and comment he volleyed, I knew he was right—there was more work to be done to verify our relation. I was operating on the assumption that he was my biological father based on the facts Ann had given. I was speculating that he was actually the guy, but I had no definitive proof. And paternity can always be questioned.

After our phone call, I told Michele that I had reached out to Mr. H. because I felt an urge to meet him before the chance to do so was gone forever. We were together in my car when Mr. H. called again. I looked at Michele, flashed the screen of my phone to her so she would know who was calling, and made a facial expression with rolling eyes that said, "Well, this oughta be good." I answered and put it on speakerphone so Michele could hear him, too. I had described his overbearing conversational style and tone to her before, so this was her chance to hear the man for herself.

He called with the exciting news that he had a great idea. We had already agreed to a DNA test and I was going to try to access my original birth certificate, so what other great idea could he have? I listened closely as he said, "Why don't we go on television? We can go on the Maury Povich show, do a DNA test, and reveal the results on TV!" I immediately rolled my eyes in disgust at that ridiculous, attention-seeking idea, and truly bit my tongue to stop myself from blurting out, "That's the dumbest thing I've ever heard!" I looked at Michele in disbelief with my mouth wide open and a WTF look in my eyes. She shook her head calmly, trying to silently extinguish the flames of my irritation. She whispered, "Just tell him you'll think about it." She was right. He thought it was a good idea, and there was no point trying to argue him down in the moment of his highest excitement. When I hung up the phone, Michele and I discussed the idea to try to surmise why he would spew such a ridiculous proposal. She pointed out that the ploy could have been an attempt to call my bluff on doing a DNA test. Maybe he thought I would shy away from a television appearance, then he could claim that I was the one to retreat from doing the test. Even though attention-seeking was not my goal, I would not be deterred that easily. The whole thing reminded me of the request from *The Montel Williams Show*. I'll bet he was really hoping that episode would air back then for his 15 minutes of fame; this request was a second chance at the limelight.

During our vacation in St. Vincent, I went online and ordered an AncestryDNA test for Mr. H. When we returned home from vacation, the DNA test was in our mailbox. With AncestryDNA, the process begins by going to their website and logging in specific, identifying information for your particular DNA test so that it may be tracked throughout the course of its journey. I opened it and activated it online, attaching the tracking code to my own Ancestry account. Even though I immediately activated the test online, I procrastinated on mailing the test to him. Life got in the way when we returned from vacation, and it didn't seem very urgent to get the testing kit out the door immediately.

A week after I activated Mr. H's DNA test online, I received an envelope in the mail from Mr. H. Inside was another photocopy of a black and white picture of himself at his desk, with some scripture written on it. I'm not a religious person, so I don't necessarily identify with those kinds of writings and I wasn't able to decipher the meaning of his chosen scripture. I skimmed it, then nonchalantly handed it to Michele. She read it, but she wasn't able to make any sense of it either. Being the smart woman that she is, she flipped the page over to the back, where she found a handwritten note. After she read it, she said under her breath, "Oh no."

"OK, give it back. Let me see," I said, my hand outstretched. On the back of the grainy photocopied scripture was a handwritten message to me, dated April 16, 2017.

Mr. Davis, You are not related to me! Sympathetically, Mr. H.

I was stunned. Michele said that the look on my face was that of a child who had just received some disappointing news. I quickly covered my emotions with a flip comment. "It's OK, I don't really care." But I had overstated my callousness toward the final proclamation from Mr. H. I did care. How could he know so definitively that we were not related? This guy was supposed to be my biological father. How could he just reject me like this, with no explanation? I couldn't believe he didn't even want to meet me. Later that day, I admitted my false bravado in that moment to Michele.

So, I picked myself up, drove to the post office around the corner from my house, and sent the Ancestry DNA test to Mr. H certified mail. I figured I had already purchased the kit and he already agreed to take the test, so there was no reason not to proceed.

When I left the post office, I sent Mr. H a text to let him know that I had received his note, his DNA test was already in the mail, and that I hoped he would at least submit his DNA sample for confirmation. I knew that if the results came back negative for a DNA match between us, we could officially close our relationship.

I checked the certified mail status online, verifying that Mr. H. had received the package. I went online to AncestryDNA a few times to see if he had submitted his DNA sample, but he never did. I never heard from Mr. H. again.

In the days that followed, I tried to be OK with the fact that I had no other leads on whom my biological father could be. It was impossible to name another candidate without Ann, and she was gone. I guessed I had reached the end of the road. I had been incredibly fortunate to have lived a storybook reunion with her. The pendulum had swung in the opposite direction to a more bitter experience with Mr. H., and things had settled back in the middle. I had a 50% success rate reuniting with my birth parents, and it would have to be enough. Whomever my biological father was, his identity would remain a mystery.

CHAPTER 14

"Many a mile has been traversed and there are miles to go."

I SETTLED INTO THE NOTION that my adoption journey was over, reconciling myself to the fact that my life would be focused on the family and friends who already surrounded me and I knew loved me. Interestingly, our focus had shifted to Michele's family and their genealogical journey. Like so many other families, Michele's also had mysteries waiting to be revealed. Michele's mother, Susan, is also an adoptee—but unlike me, she never had any desire to search for her birth family. Therefore, her heredity, genetics, and lineage were completely unknown to the family. She said none of those details about herself had ever interested her. However, Susan's youngest daughter Stephanie, who was in her late 20s at the time, was really curious about her mother's background because, of course, it was also her own.

Stephanie is an inquisitive woman raised in the internet age, so any question she has ever had can usually be answered with a quick internet search. When it occurred to her that she had questions about her heredity and that consumer availability of DNA testing could open doors to satisfy her curiosities, she was all in. When ideas pop into her head,

Stephanie's energy and enthusiasm for cool new projects and unusual experiences can be infectious; Michele's interest in DNA testing was sparked as well. Curiosity grew between Susan's daughters about how much they were genetically alike and how much they're different. In every family, there are unique, sometimes astonishing facts revealed in the results of genetic testing, and our family was on a path to discover part of its true heritage too.

Michele could make a few basic assumptions about her Caribbean descent and the likelihood of some of her paternal roots going back to Africa. But her mother's heritage was a complete mystery. Susan is white and grew up in Montreal, Canada. Fredrick is black and from the Caribbean, and their children Michele, Marcus, and Carl all have the unique appearance that many biracial people have. Their skin is light brown, and their hair is thicker than the texture of Caucasian hair but not as thick as the hair of people with two parents of African descent. Michele struggled a little bit with her interracial identity growing up. White people saw her as black, black people saw her as white, and Latinos frequently try to speak with her in Spanish.

After Susan and Fredrick's divorce in the early 1970s, Susan married another doctor, also named Fred, who is Stephanie's dad. So, this round of DNA testing would be an interesting genealogical investigation with myriad questions being answered simultaneously, like: What is Susan's genealogical heritage? In what ethnic ways were Stephanie and Michele related to each other, and how were they different? How prevalent was the DNA of each of their respective fathers, Fredrick and Fred? And, of course, how much DNA did Seth get from everyone who contributed? He had the blood of Susan, Fredrick, Ann, and...an unidentified man.

I was most curious about Seth's heritage, because I got answers about my own right after I met Ann. In 2010, while on a work trip to Silicon Valley my new boss, then HHS CTO Bryan Sivak, and I had a meeting in the offices of 23andMe. Ann Wojcicki, co-founder and CEO, causally handed me one of their DNA tests to submit later. After the trip,

I returned to Maryland and got Ann to submit a sample too, mostly for the novelty of confirming that we were mother and child. When an adoptee finds their parent, even if they can plainly see that they are kin to each other and definitely connected, it's still reassuring to see scientific proof that you're related. But that meant the novelty of seeing my DNA test results had worn off years earlier. 23andMe confirmed that I was 63.5% Sub-Saharan African (mostly West African) and 34.5% European (large parts British & Irish). The lingering question of whether there was any "white" in my family had been clearly answered in the affirmative. Later, I would learn there was more "White" in my background than I realized.

Michele, Seth, and I submitted our AncestryDNA tests in the spring of 2017. On May 2, I received an email that the DNA results were complete, and I could log in to Ancestry.com to review them. Of course, I assumed my results were a duplicate of what I already knew from my 23andMe test, so I only poked around online a little bit. I didn't nerd out in the details from this second round of tests. Two weeks later, I got the email confirming Seth's and Michele's results were available too; that was the really interesting stuff to me.

The results showed that Michele's most dominant traits were 27% Great Britain, 22% West African, 9% Western European, and 10% Ashkenazi Jewish. Her interracial heritage created a fascinating mix, and completely surprised us with her Ashkenazi Jewish heritage. Seth's DNA is mostly divided between 43% West African and 29% Great Britain.

AncestryDNA does a very nice job of visualizing a person's genetic heritage on a world map, chronicling the migration of people from place to place throughout history. I could see a general visualization of how Michele's genealogy formed over centuries of human migration. It was cool to see historical facts about various periods in global history, along with interesting tidbits I had simply glossed over when I perused my own results. I decided to go back to my results to dig a little deeper and see my own visualizations.

Who Am I Really?

I studied the path of my people, transplanted from the Benin/Togo area of Africa through the islands of the Caribbean to the American South. Of course, I already knew most of those facts from basic American history lessons detailing the slave trade over hundreds of years. But now the facts of history were shown on my personal timeline, and the data were talking specifically about me. It was captivating.

Back when I joined 23AndMe, I found a lot of 3rd, 4th, and 5th cousins whose DNA matched mine, but none so close to me that I wanted to learn more about them or pursue a relationship. When the AncestryDNA results came back, I didn't even bother considering the DNA matches. I already knew what it would say: "You have a lot of 3rd, 4th, and 5th cousins." But I was so fascinated by the data visualization of my ancestors' journeys, I figured I should give the DNA matches a closer look. There was an outside chance I might find something mildly interesting.

The top of the screen read, *AncestryDNA Matches for Damon Davis*. Below, my DNA matches were arranged in descending order, with closest matches at the top and more distant matches down toward the bottom. My first grouping was, of course, *Parent/Child*, and of course I expected to see Seth and my DNA match there. To my great surprise, the Parent/Child section had two entries. Two?! Someone with the initials W.W. was my second parent/child relationship. What?!

I read the details closely, stunned by what I was seeing. One line read, *Possible range: Parent, Child—immediate family member*. The next said, *Confidence: Extremely High.*

But the last line left me staring at the screen in shock.

Relationship: W.W. is your father. I read it again. *W.W. is your father.*

I looked away for a second, then I read it a third time. Then again, confirming that the word was in fact *father*. I was excited and completely confused at the same time. *Holy shit*, I thought. I had found my biological father when I wasn't even looking for him. But I had no clue who he was.

That new discovery left me completely baffled. Ann had very clearly told me that my biological father was Mr. H. She was there, so I figured she must know who it was. I had read the story of her involvement with Mr. H. in my adoption papers, in which she had documented her story back in 1972. When we reunited, she told me she had no secrets, and confirmed his identity for me in 2009. Pat had told me the same story when I met her in Los Angeles. Ann's story never wavered, but now it was scientifically proven that she was wrong about my birth father's identity. I wished more than anything she was still alive, so I could reveal to her what I had learned. I'm sure we would have had a laugh!

I clicked on the *information* icon next to the DNA results to try to learn more. The pop-up window read *Amount of shared DNA: 3,376 centimorgans, shared across 105 DNA segments.* I had no clue what a centimorgan was, but 3,376 sure seemed like we shared a lot of them.

I was in a bit of shock, so I tried to think of ways to validate the results or prove AncestryDNA had gotten this wrong. I realized I had a comparative reference for my relationship to W.W.; the DNA match with Seth was right there too, so I could easily compare our shared DNA segments. I clicked on Seth's DNA match with me, and it revealed *3,401 centimorgans shared across 98 DNA segments.* It was a 25 centimorgan difference between me and W.W. and me and my own son, a differential of only 7 DNA segments. I shared more DNA segments with this stranger than I do with Seth! Any doubts about being related to him vanished. W.W. was my father. *Now, who the hell is W.W.?* I wondered.

Online DNA analytics websites offer their users a way to message one another directly when they discover a match. The decision to try to connect with a match is totally up to the user. I received several messages on 23andMe from strangers, saying they'd like to chat. Suddenly the tables were turned, and I was the one hoping my AncestryDNA message would be positively received. Whether the recipient answered my inquiry or not would determine whether or not I ever got any answers about the identity of the mystery man.

W.W.'s profile was administered by someone else; the system showed the last time they'd logged on was that same day. Cool! That meant the person was actively engaged, and there was a chance that I could connect with them. Hopefully, they would connect me with W.W.

My introductory message simply said that I was an adoptee, the match I just discovered was fascinating, and I hoped we could connect so that I could learn more.

> May 12, 2017: *I just noticed a very, very close match with an AncestryDNA account W.W. that you administer. I see your login ID also administers other related accounts that I'm also a match with. I'd like to connect to learn more about your relation, if you're interested. I'll tell you I was adopted, so I've been interested in learning more about my heritage.*

I checked for replies for several days, and I could see the administrator was logging in regularly. But there was no response.

Since the person wasn't answering, I started to feel like I might have to unravel the mystery myself. I had to start tracking down who this person was, in any way that I could. "Do you know who W.W. could be?" I asked Pat over the phone the next day. Pat recalled that Ronald Waters, the same man who shouted Ann's name on the streets of Baltimore, had a brother named Worthington Waters, or W.W. But as she thought back, Pat couldn't make sense of an intimate relationship between Ann and Worthington in her memories. Worthington was married with several children, and working as a manager at Sears in

Baltimore around the time Ann was pregnant. It was a striking coincidence that Pat knew a man with the initials W.W. whom Ann also knew, but Pat couldn't place Ann and Worthington in the same city at the time I was conceived. Pat was pretty sure Worthington Waters wasn't the guy.

Back online, I decided I would make a more impassioned plea to the person in control of W.W.'s AncestryDNA account. I needed them to truly understand the situation I found myself in, with an unexpected clue to the identity of one my natural parents. My next message had to underscore the facts of my situation, reassure them I didn't want to cause anyone harm with my emergence, and make sure it was clear that they were holding the keys to unlock the remainder of my life's mystery.

> *May 15, 2017: Hi there, just thought I would check back in with you. After a closer look, I see that you're the administrator for about 7 Ancestry accounts that I have an "extremely high" or very high DNA match with, and at least 4 where I have a "good" match.*
>
> *Again, as an adoptee, I'm completely disconnected from my heredity or any knowledge of my lineage. Therefore, I really just want some confirmation about whom I'm connected to. I have a suspicion about my biological father, a former Detroit police officer, but I have no confirmation.*
>
> *Let me reassure you, I'm really not trying to intrude into anyone's life; I'd honestly just like a quick confirmation on who the extremely high matches are in my DNA. Then, I'm happy to leave the family in peace.*
>
> *I'm not trying to stir up trouble. Just like you and yours, I have a life of my own that I cherish and will return to— hopefully with some closure, with your help, please.*

Who Am I Really?

If you'd like, you can check me out in the following places:

https://about.me/damondavis

https://www.facebook.com/damon.l.davis

If you'd like to chat further, please feel free to call me at 301-xxx-xxxx, or email me at m_____n@gmail.com.

Hope to hear from you soon,

Damon

That weekend, Michele, Seth, and I were driving around in my SUV, trying to get Seth to take a nap in the car before a big night out. As soon as he fell asleep in the backseat, the phone rang; it was a number from Kentucky that I didn't recognize. I normally don't answer unidentified callers, but Ancestry DNA had revealed that people on W.W.'s family tree were also from Kentucky, so I pulled over to answer the phone.

A woman's voice filled the car and Michele listened in. The conversation began tentatively, with us feeling each other out. The woman was careful not to identify herself, telling me that I had been messaging her daughter online about a genetic connection. I wasn't sure how receptive she was to my outreach, so I knew it was important to be honest and transparent. I explained my adoption journey to that point, talked about my reunification with Ann to add some emotional emphasis to the story, and ended with the amazing coincidence of finding a paternal match on AncestryDNA. When I finished my story, I paused and asked her if I could at least have her first name, because I still had no clue whom I was talking to. She told us her name was Pam.

She asked me to tell her what I thought I knew about my biological father. I shared that I'd been told he was a Detroit Police officer, and it was in that city where I was conceived. Pam said my biological father was never a cop. "I know your father. I've met him, and he doesn't think he has any children," she added. *Well, this news is going to be a big shock*, I thought.

Pam was feeling more comfortable, so she opened up a bit about who she was and how all of this happened. Their family, Caucasian and living in the south, were tracing her husband's lineage all the way back to slave ownership, doing DNA testing along the way to confirm genetic relationships. The test results had revealed that he had relatives in the African-American community. The African-American bloodline traced all the way back to the days of slavery as well. It sounded like they hadn't anticipated a cross-pollination in their lineage, and it really sparked their curiosity to learn more about where the genetic pools blended together. They knew that identifying the specific slave who had produced children from the slave owner required more DNA testing and deep research of historical records. Pam's family offered to pay for DNA tests for suspected relatives on the family tree, hoping that a larger pool of people would begin filling in the puzzle pieces. They had completed over 80 DNA tests, and guess whose DNA was among them? W.W.

In an awesome coincidence, Pam said they were going to a family reunion the very next weekend, where they expected to see W.W. She joked that her family were likely be the only Caucasian people at a family reunion full of African-American family members. Pam pledged to talk with him about this development and gauge his receptivity to the news that he had fathered a child 44 years earlier.

The weekend of the reunion came, and ironically, I accidentally dialed Pam while they were en route to the big event. I was completely embarrassed because I didn't want her to think I was stalking her for answers. We had a great conversation and they accepted my profuse apology for calling. But after the reunion, I didn't hear anything from Pam.

I played it cool at first, but then I was kinda stunned. Surely, she knew how important it was to me to hear an update on W.W. I wondered why she hadn't been in touch, but I figured she'd experienced a lot at the family reunion, and I was sure there was plenty for her to do to get back to her own life afterward. Giving her space, I waited a few weeks before I reached out to check in.

During that down time, waiting for W.W. to feel comfortable enough to contact me through Pam, Michele's cousin Damien messaged me through Ancestry.com. We chatted about his work to chronicle Michele's paternal side of the family, and I shared my work to document my biological family. He suggested I try a site called GEDMatch to augment my work. It provides genealogical analysis tools you can use once you've uploaded your DNA file. Honestly, I couldn't imagine engaging with another online platform about my DNA. I already confirmed my connection to Ann on 23andme and learned about my genetic makeup. I was in disbelief over my random luck to connect to this W.W. person on AncestryDNA. There was nothing more I could learn from this GEDMatch site, I was sure. I politely told Damien I'd check it out, but I didn't prioritize it at all.

The summer of 2017 was marching on with the mystery of W.W.'s identity still unsolved, but I was patient. Late one night in June, I decided to log into GEDMatch to check it out for myself. The site allowed me to automatically download my 23&Me DNA data file and upload it to GEDMatch for analysis. When the upload was complete, GEDMatch returned a message saying its analysis could take 24 hours. In this digital age of immediate, automated responses to my wildest queries online, the 24-hour estimated response time was an eternity. As quickly as the idea struck me to log into GEDMatch, I was off to something else online, figuring I'd get back to it whenever.

On July 10, I was in Michele's office in D.C., reading about an employment opportunity online, when I decided my brain needed a break. I leaned back in my chair with a yawn and a big stretch in the glow of the warm afternoon sun filling the small conference room. Then it randomly hit me that I still hadn't re-checked my GEDMatch results. I logged into the site with curiosity about what it had to offer, because I had never heard of it before I spoke to Damien. I was ready to have a little fun poking around and learning.

I clicked *one-to-many comparison*, expecting to see a bunch of 4th and 5th cousin matches. There he was again; my highest DNA match was W.W. Each column of data had some technical genetic measurement that I was unfamiliar with. One column was titled *Haplogroup*, another *Autosomal*, and another *X-DNA*. I didn't know what any of that stuff meant, but I studied every data point, trying to soak them all in. But one of the last columns titled *Name*, had an unmistakable meaning. *William White*, his row read. "Holy crap, that's W.W.," I exclaimed, alone in the room. This third online DNA platform, which I almost wrote off as a waste of time, had just delivered the one piece of information I was most interested in: my biological father's name! I called Michele over to show her my computer screen, tracing my finger across his row on the way to my discovery. She saw William White's full name and smiled, putting her hand on my shoulder.

There was another column after his name, listing an email address. I wanted to email him right then, but I paused to think carefully about whether I should do so or not. One problem was I had told Pam that I would allow her the chance to speak with him first, and I wanted to honor our agreement. Even though I hadn't heard from her recently, I also didn't know if she had actually shared the news with him—or how he had received it, if so. Further, what if it wasn't even his email address? If I emailed him and an unintended recipient got the message, who didn't know I existed, it could rock his world in a way that I didn't wish upon anyone. It was Pam's family's genealogy project that had allowed me to learn W.W. was my biological father, but it was my cousin-in-law's information that led me to GEDMatch and revealed that his name was William White. It was quite a conundrum, yet somehow, reaching out to him myself didn't seem appropriate. I chose to stick to the plan I'd made with Pam to avoid creating conflict.

Who Am I Really?

I texted Pam to let her know I knew W.W.'s identity and asked if we could talk. She texted me back, confirming she had shared the news with him. She gently reminded me that my emergence was a huge development for a man who never thought he had any children his whole life, so I needed to give him time to process it all. Pam was right; there was no way to rush something this big. I had been looking for him for a long time, but he had only known I existed for a few weeks. I had to be patient, allowing him time for things to sink in.

After that call, I tried to empathize with how Mr. White could be feeling. I guessed at how I would react, if I suddenly found out I had a son that I'd had no idea existed. I wondered what I would think if I learned that a woman I had been with years earlier had given birth to my child. He must have had questions, like who my mother was, what kind of person I am, and why I was looking for him after all this time. That empathetic thought process helped me see that Ann had gotten something from me in the beginning of our reunion that Mr. White had not: an introductory letter answering all of those questions. He deserved the respect of a similar introduction, so I texted Pam to ask if she would act as our intermediary. She agreed, so I drafted a letter to Mr. White and dropped it in the mail to her.

July 15, 2017

Greetings, Mr. White,

You must be filled with so many emotions and unanswered questions since you learned that you have a son. I know this is an unexpected part of your past that you could not have anticipated, so please know that I truly empathize with your need to take time to process the news. Let me first assure you that I have only the best intentions in reaching out to you. I had an amazing reunification with Ann Sullivan, and I'm simply trying to learn more about how I came to be on this Earth. I'm perfectly healthy, happy, and well adjusted; there are no surprises waiting for you, should you choose to be in contact with me. I'm just a guy trying to learn more about his past.

I was thinking you might appreciate it if I told you a little bit about myself, sharing a bit of my journey to find Ann Sullivan, and of course the pathway to locating you. I'll be brief, as the stories are very rich and interesting, but it's also a lot to take in at once.

My full name is Damon L. Davis. I live in Silver Spring, MD, and I'm 44 years old. I'm married with one natural-born son, who is nine years old, and two older adoptees, who are 20 and 22 years old. I had two great parents in adoption who gave me a lot of love and afforded me many opportunities to grow and explore. I'm a pretty simple guy who loves to laugh and make jokes, and I generally don't take things too seriously. I'm warm and outgoing, and I generally get along with most people I meet. I've lived in the Maryland area my entire life, except during my college years at Hampton University…where Ann also went to school.

My journey to find Ann began after my wife, Michele, gave birth to our son, Seth. When he was an infant, it struck me deeply that this little person was the first blood relative I had ever known. That realization drove deeper the heartfelt bond I was making with my son when he was an infant. That revelation made me very curious about my own biological past. I reached out to Baltimore social services, through which I was adopted in 1972, to launch the search for my biological parents. They located Ann very quickly, as she was in the Baltimore area at the time and had retained her maiden name. Through our social worker as the intermediary, I wrote her an introductory letter much like this one I'm writing to you. She responded warmly with an introductory letter of her own. Once we had mutually agreed to moving forward with a reunion, our social worker put us directly in touch with one another. Talking to her by phone, I found out that she worked only two blocks from me in Washington, D.C. The very next day, which was her birthday, I went to her office to surprise her for our reunification. We developed a wonderful relationship thereafter, and I've been very thankful for our reunion ever since.

Much later, I finally decided that it was time to seek out my biological father. I had been face to face with the woman who gave me life, so I hoped to locate the man who was also part of how I came to be. Initially I connected with another man whom Ann had named as my biological father. However, during my interactions with him, I learned that my AncestryDNA results returned a very definitive DNA link to a person identified only as W.W. As you may already know, I reached out to the administrator of your AncestryDNA account, hoping to connect with you one day. Pam was kind enough to call me to explain how her family was involved in your DNA testing, maintaining her anonymity and yours during our conversation. Eventually I confirmed your identity with one of Ann's friends from the library studies program at Wayne State University.

So here we are.

As I said to Ann in my introductory letter to her, take your time. I know this is a lot to contemplate. I hope that my words have brought you some comfort and clarified some of my journey for you. I want to reassure you that I don't want or need anything from you. I'm healthy, happy, and stable in my life. I'm simply seeking a little more understanding about my past.

I'll welcome any contact you feel ready for, when the time is right for you.

I wish you all the best,

Damon L. Davis

Mailing Address: xxx, Silver Spring, MD 20910

Phone: xxx

Email: xxx

Webpage about me: http://about.me/damondavis

Again, I didn't hear from Pam for a while after I mailed the letter. I texted to check in with her, whereupon she replied that her father had been ill. Pam apologized that my correspondence with Mr. White would have to wait, as she was away from home with her family. Needless to say, having recently lost my father, I was sympathetic to what she was going through. I settled into patience and anticipation yet again.

 I found myself with plenty of time to think of ways to learn more about Mr. White. I tried to find him online, but the internet had an abundance of William Whites, and a dearth of information about anyone whom I thought I might be related to. Thinking hard about my options, I remembered that Ann had introduced me to two of her graduate school classmates, Evelyn and Sharon. Sharon was the woman who had offered

Who Am I Really?

Ann asylum in her apartment in Buffalo. Meeting them was an amazing experience, because Ann was finally able to share her full truth about the days in Detroit with them. While I was glad to meet them at the time, I was really thankful I still had their contact information after Ann's passing.

I sent Sharon a text explaining that I had new information about my biological father, asking if she had known a man named William White. "Yes, he was in school with us," she replied. Finally, I had someone on my team who knew who this guy was! We agreed to get on the phone the next day, so she could share what she recalled.

On July 11 I rode with Michele into her office, so that she could listen in on my call with Sharon. I knew there would be a lot to take in as Sharon spoke, and Michele remembers everything. First, I caught Sharon up on how I had luckily found Mr. White on Ancestry, then learned his name through GEDMatch. So, I asked her again if she knew William White; I wanted to hear her voice saying yes, not just read her affirmative answer in a text message. "Oh yeah, I knew Bill White. He was the only black male student in the library science class at Wayne State." She shared that he was a little older than her and Ann, having gone into the field of library sciences from an unrelated field of work. In those days, Bill was a Detroit resident, so he invited their crew to his house to watch football games and for holidays; he entertained the non-Detroiters on short breaks from school, as well. She said they all thought he was cool and experienced because he was older. He would say rebellious things about the program, like, "I'm not falling for any of this stuff." They all ate it up. He was the older man with sage wisdom, because he had been around. As Sharon relayed her memories, I began to see how this guy would have been attractive to Ann when she was younger.

Sharon thought Bill was married at the time, because he had a single-family home and wasn't living like a bachelor. But she was never positive about his marital status; he hung out with them a lot, but they never met his wife. Sharon couldn't recall the reason, but Bill did not complete the library sciences program. One day he simply left, according to her, and no one ever heard from him again. "It was like he just disappeared from the face of the earth."

When her story concluded, Sharon reminded me that when we'd met at Evelyn's house, she had showed me a class picture that included Ann, Evelyn, and herself. The photo was taken at the beginning of the semester, when the students barely knew one another. "Bill was in that picture too!" she exclaimed with delight. Sharon texted me a picture of the class photo, and there was Bill, standing immediately behind Ann. When I saw them, it struck me that while I was focusing on Ann and her friends in the picture the first time, I was actually holding a picture of both of my biological parents, and I didn't even know it… Ann didn't know, either. I was astonished to learn I had seen Bill's face before.

On August 4 I was in Michele's office again, where I'd learned so much about my paternal connection in recent weeks. It was there that I discovered Mr. White's full name on GEDMatch, and Sharon had familiarized me with how Ann and Bill might have connected in 1972. It was the end of a beautiful summer day, but I was trapped inside, editing the 21st episode of my podcast. Audio editing can be a laborious task, hours of listening, cutting, and splicing. But once all of the puzzle pieces are in place, the end product can be amazing. Needing to rest my ears, I took an email break. Amidst the electronic pile of junk mail that had amassed in my inbox, one email message from Mr. White stood out from them all.

Bill:

How cha do???????? Hello Damon, I received your July missive in yesterday's mail ... glad to hear from you. Like you, I have many questions but, probably not as many as you. We can chat and we will...Suggestion - make a list of questions you want answered - I'm open to all - no

Who Am I Really?

secrets!!!!! Am I anxious - NO!!! Curious-YES!!!!!!!!!!!!!!!!!!!! You have lots of cousins, nieces, and nephews. Since there is a three-hour difference in time - are evenings or weekends better for a phone chat????? Peace, love and good vibes.... Bill

Seeing William White's name in my email box was a surprise and a relief. I was so glad he had accepted my outreach and was open to chatting with me. He said there were no secrets, so I was excited to hear about his life during the time he knew Ann and learn where he'd been since then. Judging from how he expressed himself in that first email, I figured the dude must be quite a character. I wrote him a quick email back to say how great it was to hear from him, and how much he had made my day. I said I was open for a call whenever he wanted, because connecting with him was huge, and I was excited that my journey had linked us. Since he mentioned the three-hour time difference between us, I made sure to tell him that our family was traveling to Los Angeles for a whole week. I hoped that somehow, he was there too…or at least nearby, and that we could meet.

The next day Bill sent two more emails, but his information was trickling in slowly. Every time I saw his name in my email inbox, I smiled and felt just a little bit lighter. In the second message, he rattled off some basic stats about himself, including his birthdate in 1932, the fact that he was married, and that he lived in Las Vegas. When our family traveled to Los Angeles for our annual end of summer trip, we would fly right over his house; when we landed, we would be only a short flight away. But I was getting ahead of myself, thinking that we might meet so soon after that first email.

The third email had only one line, "I just read your tribute to Ann. I'm happy you found me," he said. I read it repeatedly. Bill said he was happy I'd found him! That meant a lot. I wished I could have told him myself that Ann was gone, but it was good that he was aware—and since he'd read my remarks, in a way he *did* hear the news from me.

I emailed Bill early in the afternoon. He had asked me to send over a list of questions, but I resisted emailing my questions. There was just so much we had to say to one another, and I wanted to talk with him by phone, getting a sense of how he was feeling. When a person reads an email, they can't hear the sender's tone of voice conveying excitement, disappointment, or bewilderment. I wanted to hear this guy's voice. Still, if that was how he wanted to proceed, I would honor his request. I started small, with just three questions: Where are you from originally? What did you feel when Pam told you the news? and Why did you leave the library sciences program at Wayne State?

But I also made it clear that I really wanted to talk. He was only answering emails once a day, and it just wasn't enough for me, given the gravity of our situation and the ubiquity of modern communications technology. I was excited, and in this modern day, I knew we could be in touch way more often. I said, "Of course, as a young guy I'm on my mobile device quite often, but the most interesting information I can get from it these days is coming from you. I'm glad to be in touch, and I look forward to your responses daily." I sent the signal that I really wanted to chat more if he was up for it, but I didn't want to force him to engage with me.

He replied with an email sharing his phone number, offering to chat. Excellent! He was willing, and I was definitely going to call. There was plenty to do before we left for Los Angeles the next day, but everything could wait for me to make that call.

That night, I unlocked my back door and went out on our deck again. It was the same place where I had spoken with Ann for the first time, so I thought it was appropriate to have my first call with Bill there, too. I don't normally get nervous going into a situation, but I definitely felt the excitement for a conversation with my biological father—who, until very recently, didn't even know he was a father. I sat in my deck chair, relaxed, and dialed his number. His phone rang a few times, then the answering machine picked up. I was a little disappointed, but I started to leave a message anyway when the automated voice was interrupted by a man's voice saying, "Hello?" It was Bill. I didn't know what to say, so I admitted I was a little nervous. He assured me I didn't have anything to be nervous about, and warmly told me that he was looking forward to hearing how I made my way to him. I started by telling the story of Seth's birth and my amazing reunification with Ann. I shared the details of my failed connection with Mr. H, whom Ann had named as my biological father, and how Michele's family's genealogy project led me to him. He listened attentively to everything. At times, the phone line was completely silent when I stopped talking. I had to ask if he was still there, and thankfully he was.

We laughed a lot during that first conversation, and I appreciated his silliness. If light-hearted levity is a trait you can pass down to your child, I may have gotten some of that from Bill.

I asked him if he had any other children. He said, "Not that I know of." I burst out in laughter. That was the same answer my Dad always gave when people asked if I was his only son, or if he had other children. And of course, there was the irony that if someone else had asked Bill the same question a few weeks before, his answer would have been the same; he didn't know I existed yet.

When I finished, it was Bill's turn. At 85 years old, he still has a very sharp mind and his voice sounded strong on the phone. He explained in more detail how he was related to Pam's family, which I was eager to hear. Were it not for their family's project to discover more of their own history, Bill's DNA would never have been online and available to link with mine. He explained that he was a cousin of Pam's husband, by way of a slave owner. They discovered the slave owner, George S. Hoard, had about 18 slaves, but the vast majority of them were mulatto: mixed black and white. Based on their research into slave records, about 16 of the slaves were much younger than the oldest slaves. Their ages suggested they were the mulatto offspring of the slave owner, and Bill's grandfather, John Henry Hoard, was among them.

We divulged a lot of information during that first conversation; there was a lot for both of us to think about. When our chat was winding down, Bill verified with me that our family was leaving for the West coast the next day. I confirmed it, jokingly saying, "We'll be in your time zone," hoping he was interested in meeting me. He said, "Let's continue to talk. We'll come up with something. You'll be too close, and for a long time." It was really cool to hear Bill suggest that he wanted to meet me during my trip to L.A. It was a really nice affirmation, and I left our conversation feeling like things were going to be good.

One Sunday in Los Angeles, I was sitting on the steps of Susan's pool deck, taking in the southern California sun. Michele extended our stay in Los Angeles, so that we could make the trip to Las Vegas to meet Bill. Michele came outside and asked how I was feeling before our meeting. I said, "I feel good that a mystery has been solved. I wouldn't call it closure… It just feels good to have the final piece to the puzzle." I explained that the situation with Bill was very different than my reunification with Ann. Lee had read Ann's letter to me over the phone, her birthday was the next day, and I sprang into action to surprise her for our first meeting. It all unfolded so fast with her that there was no time to think or overthink; I just reacted.

Meeting Bill already had more anticipation involved, because the timeline was longer. I had already spoken to him several times and had gotten to know just a little about him. It was incredibly fortuitous that we already had a trip planned out West at the same time I was connecting with Bill for the first time. I connected with Ann so quickly that the experience had spoiled me for wanting the same expeditious reunion with Bill. It would have been difficult for me to have to wait weeks or months before meeting him.

As I sat there anticipating our reunion, I wondered how things would go. What would the first moments be like? How does a man who's lived 85 years on Earth suddenly receive another guy who is his son, and whom he didn't even know he'd conceived 44 years before? Ann knew definitively that I was out there, and hoped I would find her again one day. Bill had no idea I was coming before I found him.

On Wednesday August 16, 2017, Michele, Seth, and I boarded a plane at Bob Hope Burbank Airport for Las Vegas. The flight was very short, and as quickly as we reached our cruising altitude, it seemed like we were already descending for landing. On approach, Seth and I peered out the window together, taking in the sights. Las Vegas is the largest city in the Mojave Desert, and its suburbs sprawl for miles around the main tourist attractions on the Las Vegas Strip. Seth was busy taking in the sights of the humungous hotels and the bright lights that entertain children of every age. I was reflecting on how many times I had been to Vegas in my adult life for bachelor parties, industry conferences, and Michele's 50th birthday. My biological father was living in that city during many of those trips.

When we landed, I was excited, but mostly curious. Bill didn't have a mobile phone at the time, so I couldn't call him to easily locate him. Before the trip, I asked him how I would find him at the airport if he didn't have a phone. He said, "Oh don't worry; I'll be the guy with the blue blinking nose and the red clown shoes!" I cracked up laughing when he said it—but now I had to actually find him, and I was certain he wasn't dressed at all the way he'd described.

In the Las Vegas airport, passengers from arriving flights descend a long escalator to the baggage claim level, and you can see the entire landscape of baggage belts in front of you. As we rode down, I scanned the vastness of the floor space, wondering how we were going to find this guy and hoping I could identify him first before he saw me. I might have snuck up on him, but I had no clue who I was looking for. I made a cautious approach to the baggage claim belt for our flight, trying to see every person we passed as I searched.

We had taken our time getting downstairs, stopping to get Seth something to eat before meeting Bill. We wanted to be sure he wouldn't suddenly be "hangry" (hungry + angry) and lose control of his mood and emotions. The baggage belt for our flight was empty and all the other passengers had already left when we arrived. As we got closer, I noticed an older black man sitting alone on an adjacent baggage belt. He wasn't passing the time with his face down on a mobile phone, like most people do when there's a moment of silence in our lives. He was just calmly looking around. I knew it had to be him.

I walked over to the gentleman, passing in front of him as I asked, "Are you Bill?" He cocked his head to the side glancing up at me briefly. He didn't say a word. I almost enquired again because I didn't think he heard me. But before I could speak, he leaned over to his left and reached in his back-right pocket to retrieve his wallet. I watched with bewilderment as he opened it, pulled out his driver's license, and read his own name to himself. He looked up at me again with a sly grin and said, "Yes, I am!" Bill White stood up slowly and extended his arms for a hug that pulled me in close and tight. His strong greeting reassured me that things were going to be just fine. Bill was glad to meet me, and I was so glad to have found him. He asked me how I was feeling, and I said, "I'm great now that I'm here with you!" He smiled and nodded in agreement.

Leaving the airport, Bill and I walked together, with Michele and Seth trailing behind. They were letting us have our first moments alone, happy to be part of the experience. Michele told me later that as we walked, Seth tugged at her sleeve and whispered through welling eyes, "Mom, I'm freakin' out right now!" Meeting Bill was huge for Seth, too. It had been a year and a half since Willie's passing, and there we were, introducing him to another grandfather.

Bill drove us to his home in the northwest suburbs of Las Vegas. It was a very nice neighborhood, but like most neighborhoods, the houses looked the same. Every home was painted in an earth tone that mimicked the colors in the surrounding desert landscape. But one house stood out from the rest, with brighter colors coating its architectural accents. I was about to comment about how that particular home was so distinctive from the rest when we stopped in front of it. The most unique home on the block was Bill's, naturally.

Inside Bill's house, Seth made himself right at home. He immediately kicked his shoes off by the front door, then sprawled out effortlessly in Bill's reclining arm chair. Michele and I sat with Bill at his kitchen table, where he had assembled books of his genealogical work on our family. Each book chronicled our lineage down his maternal and paternal lines, from the days just after slavery to modern family reunions. I knew Bill less than an hour, but he was able to transport me back through time using pictures and stories about our distant relatives, with fascinating detail. As a seasoned genealogical researcher, he had documented the whole family tree, noting every birth, death, and marriage next to each historical photo. It was a lot to take in, so I pulled out my phone and took photos of his photos and their accompanying notes about each person.

Michele watched with amazement as my entire family history unfolded before my eyes. She joked that I learned more about my paternal family history in one afternoon than she's known her whole life. She was right, and I felt lucky for it. So many people wish they knew more about their family tree, and struggle to discover new branches.

I asked Bill what had inspired him to get into genealogy. He told us his own father, Bill White, Sr., never, ever talked about his family, which made Bill very curious about his paternal roots. He started researching them, uncovering his history, and developing genealogical research skills along the way. Staff members at the libraries where he dug into the past took note of his investigative prowess and began referring others who were researching their own families to him.

I couldn't believe the coincidence that both Ann and Bill were deeply fixated on genealogy, setting me up with a wealth of knowledge when I reunited with them respectively. Many times, when we become parents ourselves, we talk about the knowledge we'd like to impart to our children. Of course, my birth parents' work to record our family's genealogy benefited their entire families before my arrival—but each of them only had one son to whom they could bestow their knowledge: lucky, lucky me.

Bill recounted his research trip to Hopkinsville, Kentucky to meet Pam and her husband in November 2015. He shared more of the story of George S. Hoard, the slave owner whom we were all linked to, as well. Bill told stories of our slave ancestry and the strong evidence that Hoard had relations with at least one unknown slave, beginning the branches of our family tree, our ancestors.

Concluding the story of his trip to Kentucky, Bill shared that he had started feeling ill right before his return flight to Las Vegas. His energy had faded dramatically that day. When he arrived at the airport for his flight, he had to request a wheel chair to transport him to his departure gate. On the flight home, his peripheral vision turned black and he felt terrible. The next morning at home, he wasn't able to raise himself out of bed, so his wife, Alice, took him to the hospital where he remained for 13 days. His doctors told him that he was very lucky to be alive, because the darkening of his vision was a symptom of a blood clot moving through his system. He'd had a pulmonary embolism. That life-threatening event in his 80s made him reluctant to travel anymore. That's why Bill and Pam never connected at the family reunion; traveling and developing another clot might have meant his demise. Pam was forced to call him during her car ride home after the family reunion to tell him about me. Bill White had nearly died two years before we all sat at his dining room table meeting one another. After hearing that story, I felt even more fortunate to have met him.

Who Am I Really?

We returned to the books containing our family history and our trip down the family tree, but it was Bill whom I was most interested in hearing more about. I eagerly anticipated seeing photos from his younger days, so when we hit that point in our timeline, it was exciting. The photos that stood out were from his time in the U.S. Air Force, "Four years, eleven months, and twenty-nine days," he said. His headshot was that of young handsome man in a blue Air Force uniform, complete with hat and bomber jacket. The photo reminded me of Dad's USAF head shot. I thought it was cool that they had both been Air Force men. The notes next to another military photo said *Lackland Air Force Base,* which is in San Antonio, Texas. Willie had also passed through Lackland for basic training, roughly 10 years after Bill.

In the quiet moments between looking at youthful pictures of him in the book, I found myself staring at Bill's face in real life, there at the table. I was searching for pieces of me, imagining myself at his age. He still had a full head of hair, mostly grey with hints of black. His face had no wrinkles, though. It was amazing.

Eventually, we took a break from looking at old photos and storytelling. Michele asked him about his wife's reaction to the whole situation. "What did Alice say when you told her?" she enquired. He said he hadn't told her the news yet. Bill explained that Alice had been away from their home caring for her son for six weeks. He had needed help after shoulder surgery and during an intensive, in-home physical rehabilitation regimen. Therefore, Alice wasn't home when my introductory letter arrived in their mailbox, nor for our first few calls, and she wasn't present that day we met for the first time. In my head, I knew he was right not to tell her over the phone. Informing your wife that you have a son from 44 years prior is a face-to-face conversation, if there ever was one. There would be explaining to do, emotions to acknowledge and manage, and mental processing that had to be done together. Michele pointed out for Bill that from a woman's perspective, the news would be easier to take if he could make her feel comfortable that my conception occurred well before they met. Bill nodded his head in agreement. Still, I felt an uneasy sense of deception sitting in their home. I'm sure Alice would have liked to have known that Bill had invited his long-lost son over for the first time. But the timing just wasn't right for her to be forewarned. It was pure coincidence that our vacation to Los Angeles coincided with her trip to Michigan, and there was nothing anyone could do about it. The opportunity to meet Bill could not be passed up.

Unfortunately, time flies when you're meeting your birth father; we had to catch a return flight to Los Angeles that afternoon. Of course, Seth requested lunch at his favorite place out West, In-N-Out Burger. I wanted him to have fond memories of his time with Grandpa Bill, and lunch together was a great way to end things.

After we ate our burgers, Bill drove us to the airport and we made light conversation along the way. In a quiet moment in the car, he seemed to speak one of his inner thoughts out loud. "She didn't tell anyone she was pregnant. She must have felt so alone. I wish I would have known," he said. He wore his empathy on his sleeve, and I was glad he had shared his feelings out loud. He expressed a sensitivity for Ann's position that I really appreciated.

Bill pulled over to the curb at the airport to drop us off. Standing in the loading zone, Michele, Seth, and I gave him one final farewell hug each. We stepped up onto the curb, waving goodbyes over our shoulders. Then I remembered Sharon telling me she thought Bill was married when he was in Detroit, but she'd never seen a wife. I turned around to ask one final question. "Hey, one more thing: Were you married at the time?" Without hesitation he said, "Yes." He paused and added "Well…she was, but I wasn't." I knew he meant that in his mind his marriage was already over, and I didn't judge him for it at all. I told him I understood, and that these things happen. We smiled at each other, waved farewell, and parted ways.

Who Am I Really?

Sitting at the gate, I drafted Bill a quick email to express my thanks for a great day, and my heartfelt appreciation for his openness to meeting me:

> *Michele, Seth, and I want to sincerely thank you for a wonderful day. I feel really fulfilled having met you face to face. It was fascinating to scan your face to look for pieces of me.*
>
> *Thanks for picking us up at the airport, your hospitality, openness, and transparency, and for lunch!!*
>
> *I'll definitely be in touch. In the meantime, attached are some photos from the day.*
>
> *All the best, Grandpa Bill,*
>
> *Damon*

"Many a mile has been traversed and there are miles to go… As James Brown sang, *'I Feel Good!!!!!!'*" he replied. I felt good too! The mystery of his identity had been solved. The misery of the rejection levied by Mr. H was completely overshadowed by Bill's willingness to meeting me, openness to sharing his own story, and welcoming us into his home.

I called him to say we were home safely. During our brief phone call, Bill thanked me for having the courage to step forward. He said it was a day that would live on in his memory.

CHAPTER 15

END

ONE FRIDAY IN LATE AUGUST 2017, 45 years after Ann Sullivan and I were separated when I was born, my mind wandered from editing an episode of the *Who Am I Really?* podcast to my recent incredible experience meeting Bill. Replaying the adventure in my mind, I sat there feeling so fortunate and fulfilled that soon I began rehashing the totality of how incredibly lucky I had been throughout my life: as an adoptee, as a parent, and in reunion with my biological parents. My Mom and Dad, Veronica and Willie, were two loving parents who molded me into a pretty decent guy with a solid foundation in Columbia, Maryland. Michele and I had been so fortunate that we could provide a home for Sam and Carisssa and had conceived our son Seth naturally. When I was ready to find Ann, she was easily identifiable, open-hearted, and receptive to my return, as well as being geographically so close that we could easily form a deep, meaningful bond. And Bill, a man who didn't even know I existed, welcomed me into his home, empathized with Ann's story, and met his grandson.

Since I was sitting in front of my computer in those moments of reflection, I decided to revisit Ancestry.com to review my family tree and imagine how it would expand with all of the new information I then possessed. Shortly after meeting Ann, she had gifted her handwritten genealogy research to me. Naturally, I wanted to transcribe her body of work into Ancestry.com, but I was vexed by a problem that I never solved—and it had resurfaced after meeting Bill. The problem was how to add Ann and Bill's extensive genealogical research and historical discoveries to my existing family tree, without digitally wiping out or disrespecting the relationships that I had grown up with in adoption. For example, Willie and Veronica were listed as my parents, but the reality was I had four parents: those who raised me, and those I am genetically related to. But there was no way to show two mothers and two fathers for one person online. I really wanted to be able to visualize my whole story, the complete picture, with all the family trees that I'm connected to, documented online for posterity. My journey has been one of four families. Then it hit me: I could simply have two trees!

I quickly changed the name of my original family tree to read *Damon Davis, Adopted.* Then, I created a second online family tree, titled *Damon Davis, Biological.* I was really excited, so I quickly entered my name and birthday as the first person on the new tree. Then I added Bill and Ann's names as my parents above mine, immediately feeling a sense of peace as I looked at their names above my own. Next, I searched the photos and notes in my phone from my recent visit with Bill, then feverishly typed in the people, dates, and places applicable to them all. As I entered his mother's and father's names and their mother's and father's names, the tree blossomed on my screen. It was late into the evening when I finally finished. I went upstairs to bed, content with the notion that two full family trees online would be a more accurate reflection of reality.

The next night, I was on my laptop in bed with the big purple album open by my side. I was diligently reading the documents, then adding more branches to my family tree for grandparents, aunts and uncles, and cousins. Seth, ever the curious little dude, peeked over to see what I was doing.

"Family tree, huh?" he said with a hint of curiosity.

"Yep. It's your family tree too, actually," I said with a little more excitement hoping to spark his interest.

"It is?" he asked, abandoning the iPad. He leaned over for a better view of my screen.

"Sure is... See? Look, that's me, right there, and that's Grandma Ann and Grandpa Bill. You know what? I don't have you here on our tree yet. Let's add your name right there, under mine," I pointed to his place on the tree. He watched attentively as I typed his name, then I jokingly asked when his birthday was.

"You know when my birthday was, you were there!" He was right about that!

When I pressed *Save*, his place on the second family tree was official. I really liked seeing his grandparents above me, and his name below mine. Next, I pointed to Bill's father and said, "That's your great-grandfather!"

"Wow! Well, who is that?!" he asked excitedly. His interest in his family tree had been piqued.

Thinking about the relative he was pointing to, I rolled my eyes up toward the ceiling, making a thinking face trying to make sure I got the answer right. "That's your...great-granduncle," I declared. "And that's your great-great- great-grandfather." I took in the moment as it happened. Seth, the first blood relative I had ever known, was genuinely interested in seeing our family tree: a tree that I became more curious about after his birth, a well-documented tree researched by my biological parents, who, coincidentally, were both genealogists. Biological parents who each only had one child to pass the tree down to: me.

When Seth and I were done examining the new family tree, I closed my laptop and drifted off to sleep, feeling a sense of accomplishment. I had proven myself brave enough to take on the adventure of finding my family. I had faced the fears of learning the truth about why I was placed for adoption. I fought through the uncertainties of possibly facing secondary rejection, finding birth parents whom I didn't feel a connection with—or learning that they might be deceased. I finally had my answers, and I felt a wholeness that I didn't know I was missing until this adventure started.

Within seconds of my first breath on October 14, 1972, I was separated from the woman who had carried me for nine months. The plans were for us to live separate lives, but no one ever said that I couldn't try to find her again one day. I'm so thankful that I did; meeting Ann answered so many questions and introduced new curiosities about my biological father's identity. Trying to find him led me down a false path at first, but I learned that everyone makes mistakes; the misidentification of my birth father had been one of Ann's. Incredibly, a stroke of pure luck helped me finally find Bill.

If you're an adoptee, I hope you know that you do have the inner strength to face the truth about the circumstances for your own adoption. I've spoken to so many adoptees on the podcast who've searched for years for their answers. Most of them have said that no matter the outcome, they're glad they searched for their relatives, because living with the answers to the questions of their life is better than living with no answers at all. If you're thinking of starting your search, or you've already embarked on your voyage of discovery, I hope you find your answers to the existential question many adoptees ask themselves:

Who am I really?

***

EPILOGUE

Turning My Journey into Purpose

IN MARCH 2017, Michele, Seth, and I were on a road trip down from Washington, D.C. to Richmond, Virginia. Occasionally, we liked to visit Michele's younger siblings, Adam and Emma. Their mother, Sally Ann, has a beautiful home with a yard and a dog, two things that Seth really enjoys, and the family time is great.

Behind the wheel riding down I-95, I was listening to the *TED Radio Hour* podcast from NPR. The episode was called "Simply Happy," talking about happiness as it relates to when our minds wander. "People are substantially less happy when their minds are wandering than when they are not." After miles and miles of tree-lined highway, my mind was wandering because an idea was forming. I was reflecting on my experiences reuniting with Ann, Mr. H to that point. I was also thinking about the thousands of adoptees whose messages of joy and despair flood Facebook groups, like I AM ADOPTED, Adoption Search & Reunion, and others. I was dismayed by how seldom the entire story of an adoption is told from the adoptee's perspective.

I thought about how whenever I had the time to share my entire story of how I found Ann, the listener(s) remarked on how incredible it all sounded, that they had chills—some admitted they were about to cry.

When the listener has time to absorb the whole story, they're very moved. I was dismayed by the sometimes-abbreviated versions of other adoption stories in the local news or online. They usually lack the full color and detail of an individual's journey to find their first family. I often found myself wanting to hear what adoption was like for them growing up. I get curious about the moment when they decided they needed more information, and they wanted to search for their birth family. I also wanted to know how the reunion unfolded, and how things were for them and their newly-found family in the aftermath.

During that drive, I decided to launch the *Who Am I Really?* podcast, offering other adoptees the chance to share their *entire* story of adoption and attempts to reunite. It's their story, in their voice and in their own words. Adoptees find it cathartic to share and explore the full range of their emotions.

The stories are real, and they're fascinating in their variety and diversity. I wrote a blog post about how vastly different each adoption story can be. If you've heard one adoption story, you've only heard one unique story! To illustrate my point, I encourage you to listen to a few episodes of *Who Am I Really?*" podcast (www.whoamireallypodcast.com/episodes)

Often my guests are glad they have shared their experiences for the benefit of others who may be considering a search, are on the journey to answers, or who have found their families. Storytelling is an important part of community and culture. It is my pleasure to host the podcast, as it's a project of passion to help share a few of the millions of stories from the adoptee community.

www.ingramcontent.com/pod-product-compliance
Lightning Source LLC
Chambersburg PA
CBHW070424010526
44118CB00014B/1895